in·dulge

/in-ˈdəlj/

1. to allow oneself to enjoy the pleasure of.

Indulge

Delicious and Decadent Dishes
to Enjoy and Share

Valerie Bertinelli

HARVEST
An Imprint of WILLIAM MORROW

HarperCollins books may be purchased for educational, business, or sales promotional
use. For information, please email the Special Markets Department at SPsales@
harpercollins.com.

FIRST EDITION

Designed by Tai Blanche

Photography by John Russo

Library of Congress Cataloging-in-Publication Data has been applied for.

ISBN 978-0-06-324472-6

24 25 26 27 28   TC   10 9 8 7 6 5 4 3 2 1

Contents

1   Let's cook. Let's eat. Let's indulge.

4   In the Kitchen Again

7   Breakfast

24   A Good Day for a Sandwich

27   Sandwiches

49   Snacks & Apps

75   Salads

106   Don't Be Afraid to Ask Questions

109   Cheese & Charcuterie

114   Planning a Menu

116   Bread

133   Soups

149   Vegetables

168   Dinner for One

171   Chicken

200   Meat

218   Potatoes

230   The Best Bottle of Wine You'll Ever Have

233   Seafood

259   Pasta

278   Good Show, Ma?

281   Dessert

306   Jams, Spreads & Honeys

313   Condiments, Dressings & Sauces

338   Indulge: The Shopping List

339   Special Ingredients

340   Universal Conversion Chart

341   Index

Let's cook. Let's eat. Let's indulge.

Yes, indulge. When I think about the joys of the kitchen, the truly delicious treats that make my mouth water, I picture a bowl of fresh tomatoes, a basket overflowing with just-harvested vegetables, fruit I've picked from trees in my garden (or at the grocery store!), sticks of butter, heads of garlic, bunches of herbs—in other words, a counter full of possibilities. I also imagine soft-boiled eggs oozing rich yellow-orange yolk onto a slice of lightly toasted brioche, the Italian sub sandwiches my mom made back when I was pregnant, and the first crispy bite of my chicken parm. Of course, since I'm like most everyone else, I occasionally think about a thick hot fudge sundae topped with a sprinkle of salted peanuts and a small mountain of whipped cream, too. Hey, no shame. Only truth is spoken here.

Truth is a house specialty. For instance, I know that dietitians and therapists often frown at the word "indulge" as it relates to food, as they do words and phrases like "treat," "cheat days," and "guilty pleasure." And just as often, they tell us there are certain (seemingly ever-changing) "good" and "bad" foods that we must eat—or avoid—to be healthy. And for much of my life, I agreed. I struggled with denial, restriction, deprivation, guilt, and shame around food. No matter the meal, all I saw was a menu full of misery. I didn't pay attention to how the food I ate was prepared or tasted because I was just going to beat myself up for having eaten it. Each bite was an exercise in self-loathing. I hated myself for blowing my diet.

There's simply no way to enjoy a meal or spend any time working in the kitchen if every single step is infused with regret and judgment. I'll take it a step further. With that mindset, there is no way to enjoy your life.

I have spent more than a decade changing my relationship with food. I have asked myself questions: *How can I nourish myself, not just eat? How can I treat myself with care and compassion? How can I enjoy myself in the kitchen?* All big leaps requiring baby steps, patience, forgiveness, and a desire to grow and change. I started by reconnecting with generations of women in my family whose lives revolved around the kitchen. I opened my eyes and my heart. I learned to cook with love and infuse joy into every step of the process, just as they did.

Fourteen seasons of my own cooking show plus writing two previous cookbooks helped me evolve from obsessing about what I wasn't supposed to eat to immersing myself in the entire process of cooking, from planning and shopping and chopping and stirring to enjoying what I put on the table, whether it's for family and friends or just me dining solo. Then, as some of you know, I turned sixty and said, "Enough already." That was the final straw, the springboard to this book. I stopped getting on a scale and looking for a magic number that didn't exist. I stopped punishing myself for missing my so-called goal or slipping at lunch; I stopped rewarding myself for being "good" and punishing myself when I "cheated." I stopped counting calories. I stopped thinking of certain foods as good or bad. I quit saying no and began saying yes. And I let myself indulge.

So what do I mean when I say, "Let's indulge"? In a personal sense, I mean that I'm done expecting joy to come to me. Every day I get out of bed intent on finding it. I indulge in life. In the pleasures of being alive. It sounds simple, but it took me most of my life to get to this place, and I work hard at it. And food is one of those pleasures—an essential pleasure. This cookbook marks the journey that I—and so many of us—have taken to get to this place where I no longer deny myself and instead indulge in the entire experience of cooking and, ultimately, my desire to share what I make with those I love.

So when I say, "Let's indulge," I'm talking about everything that comes before we sit down at the table to eat. For me, being intentional about the entire process is what makes cooking so enjoyable. I love when I find a new recipe and get to shop for the ingredients. I'm discovering something I didn't know. At the store, I squeeze and smell the food I buy and imagine the flavors. Back home, I look forward to making the meal. The anticipation gives my day a lift. It beats the heck out of calculating how many calories I can afford at dinner.

When I have people over, I think about our friendship and the history we share and plan the meal accordingly. Even if it's a special occasion, the meal doesn't have to be fancy. But it can still be special. I consider their tastes and preferences, the meals we've enjoyed together in the past, and the ways I can express my feelings about them through food. Freshness. Seasonality. Herbs and spices. Setting a beautiful table. The aroma that will be wafting from the kitchen when they walk through the front door. A fun dessert. From shopping for ingredients to creating a menu that reflects my affection for my guests, cooking and eating become a deeper, more connected, more loving experience.

The more I've done this, the more I've found myself returning to memories of my grandmother and my aunts spending all afternoon in my aunt Adeline's basement kitchen and my mother making platters of food for the parties she and my dad hosted. I indulge these feelings, and my heart gets fuller.

I used to hate cooking for one. Now I think, *Who better to cook for than me?* I indulge in myself. I love eating alone now. I don't necessarily make anything fancy or complicated. A salad. A sandwich. Soup. Pasta. Instead of depriving myself, I ask, *What do I feel like? What do I want?* And because these days, as many of you know, I am frequently and delightfully the only one at the dinner table at my house, that is, if you don't count several mewing cats and a dog lying at my feet. I often find myself asking a question late in the afternoon that may sound familiar to some of you: *How much energy do I have to make dinner?*

Even when the answer is none, I say to myself, *Okay, but how do I come from a place where I am still nourishing myself in every sense of the word?*

The answer isn't complicated. When I go to the grocery store or open my refrigerator, I ask not only what I feel like but also and more important, what I need. What is my body telling me? What am I craving? How can I satisfy that need? My hope is that you will do the same and use this cookbook as inspiration. It is full of some fun, new ideas, longtime favorites, variations of family classics, and ingredients I love.

The recipes range from twists on time-tested classics to some that are a little bit fancy. But just a little bit. What all of them are is tasty, and that's by design. I want you to smell and touch the food while you're shopping. Imagine the way it is going to taste later on.

I want you to listen to the sizzle when you cook. I want you to take your time. I want you to be intentional and creative. I want you to embrace the possibilities of a counter full of fresh ingredients, the satisfaction of nourishing yourself and others, and the joy of cooking. I want you to indulge in life—your life. Stop and smell the garlic!

As you go through this book, you will see that I have all the usual mains and sides, plus a bunch of other things that are essential to my lifestyle and way of entertaining, like condiments, dressings, snacks, and irresistible desserts. You will also find notes, stories, ideas, and encouragement. I want this cookbook to be your handy go-to, like a text chain with your best friends. Open it when you're stuck for an idea that will . . . you know . . . *hit the spot.* Think of it as a direct line to me. "Hey, Val, I don't know what to make tonight. I need an idea." Or better still, "Val, I feel like doing something nice for myself. What do you think?"

Here's what I'm thinking right now: Don't save the best bite for last. Make it the first bite. Let's enjoy food. Let's enjoy our lives. Let's indulge.

And let's do it together.

In the Kitchen Again

GETTING STARTED

When you open a cookbook like this, your assumption is likely that the author is someone who spends their days in a fully stocked kitchen, with knives and spatulas at attention and waiting for their orders, stovetops crackling with melting butter and caramelizing onions, and baking pans lined up like planes on a runway ready to fly off to some fabulous destination. While that might be true of some cookbook authors, it would not be true of me these past few years when my life was consumed with disentangling myself from a broken marriage. Exhausted, I was not cooking, and when I don't cook, I don't take care of myself the way I should. I'm like so many others. Stress causes me to shut down. I get the blues. I buy premade meals. I do everything but indulge in living my best life. However, as I got into the new year of 2023, I began to not only see the light but also feel its warmth on my shoulders. Little things buoyed my spirit. I noticed strangers smiling at each other, I read about people offering tourists shelter during storms, I saw people practicing kindness. The system might be broken and the headlines depressing, but I sensed we had each other's back.

It got me excited about being kinder to myself, which led to cooking again. I began to really look forward to experimenting and playing with flavors. Don't get the idea that I immediately walked back into the kitchen and started tossing a Caesar salad or barbecuing ribs. Life is not that simple. Like everyone else, I have to work at finding inspiration. Change is gradual and requires conscious effort. While sipping my coffee, I watched mourning doves bathe joyfully in my pool. I took leisurely walks with my dog. I read amazing books. I listened to the crows and hawks squawk on their late-afternoon flyover. I laughed as my cats stared down a coyote who had found his way

into my backyard and was sitting on the other side of the living room window like a bad mood I wasn't going to let inside.

The citrus trees in my garden were full of fruit. I picked oranges, lemons, and limes and asked, *What can I do with these?* I might as well have asked, *What's something nice you can do for yourself today?* For New Year's, I bought myself a small jar of caviar and ate it with potato chips and crème fraîche. A bottle of champagne washed it down and helped send me to bed early. The next morning, I started the day with a fried egg on toast. Later, I made a grocery list. At sixty-three, I need lists for just about everything. But this was different, profound. I didn't write "sushi" and "frozen pizza." I asked what I *felt* like. What did I *want*? What did I *need*? Not what would let me get by or save me time. My body spoke to me, and I listened. I knew I'd be spoiling myself in the days ahead.

Sure enough, a few nights later, I seared a rib eye for dinner. It was just me, dinner for one, but I set the table with great care and took my time preparing the steak. My mouth watered as it sizzled. Then I did something I frequently do in a restaurant: I ate around the edges, where it was crispy and medium-rare, and saved the leftovers for lunch the next day. My next dinner was butternut squash and quinoa with a salad, over which I drizzled my lemon vinaigrette. A week or two later, I had roasted salmon and asparagus, which I mixed with quinoa and seasoned with sriracha, soy sauce, and rice vinegar. I was pleased with myself. My meals were excellent, but I got even more satisfaction from getting back in the kitchen, tending to myself with patience and love, and being creative again. That's what all of us, in our own way, do: We make things. We make lunch and dinner. We make friends. We make a life. It's not always easy. But we're worth it.

Oh, and a grocery list can also help.

BREAKFAST

"I don't do it often enough, but the day always seems to go well when I start it by indulging in something special. It puts everything else into motion."

Brown Butter Banana Walnut Muffins

The first time I made brown butter banana walnut muffins, I said, "Where have these been all my life?" The practical thing about these muffins is that you get to use the bananas that are turning brown and black and way too squishy. The flavor and crunch of the walnuts complement the bananas. And the brown butter? It just tastes so damn good.

Cooking spray (if not using
    cupcake liners)

1 stick (8 tablespoons)
    unsalted butter

1½ cups all-purpose flour

1 teaspoon baking powder

1 teaspoon baking soda

¼ teaspoon kosher salt

1 teaspoon pumpkin pie spice

3 large very ripe bananas*

½ cup packed dark
    brown sugar

2 tablespoons maple syrup

1 large egg, room temperature

2 teaspoons vanilla extract

¾ cup chopped walnuts

*If your bananas aren't ripe enough, place them on a parchment paper–lined baking sheet and bake at 300°F for 10 to 15 minutes, until the skin is completely black. Let cool to room temperature before using in the recipe.

Preheat the oven to 350°F. Spray a 12-cup muffin tin with cooking spray or use cupcake liners.

Melt the butter in a small saucepan over medium heat. Cook, stirring occasionally, until the milk solids have separated and turned a golden brown and the butter has a nutty aroma. Remove from the heat and let cool.

Whisk together the flour, baking powder, baking soda, salt, and pumpkin pie spice in a medium bowl.

In a large bowl, mash the bananas until there are no large lumps. A whisk, fork, or potato masher works well for this. Add the cooled brown butter, brown sugar, maple syrup, egg, and vanilla and whisk to combine. Next, add half of the dry ingredients, switch to a spatula, and mix until no streaks of flour remain. Repeat with the remaining dry ingredients. Fold in the walnuts.

Divide the batter evenly among the prepared muffin cups. Bake for 15 to 20 minutes, until golden brown. Let cool in the pan for 10 minutes, then use an offset spatula to transfer the muffins to a wire rack to cool completely.

Banana Cottage Cheese Pancakes

You don't need much syrup with these pancakes unless that's your preference; the vitamin-rich bananas are a sweet topping by themselves. The cottage cheese amps up the protein for those who care, like me. I've also learned a trick with these pancakes. Butter the pan generously. Then, after pouring the batter into the skillet, wait until all the bubbles pop and disappear (be patient). Then flip them. That's how you get a beautiful, crispy edge while the pancakes remain luscious and cakey inside.

1 medium banana

½ cup cottage cheese

¾ cup old-fashioned rolled oats

1 large egg

1 teaspoon baking powder

½ teaspoon ground cinnamon

2 teaspoons vanilla extract

1 tablespoon sugar

⅓ cup whole milk

Unsalted butter, for greasing

Sliced bananas, for serving

Maple syrup, for serving

Combine the banana, cottage cheese, oats, egg, baking powder, cinnamon, vanilla, sugar, and milk in a high-powered blender. Start blending on low speed, gradually increasing the speed to high, until mostly smooth. It's okay if the batter has a little texture.

Melt about 1 tablespoon of butter in a large nonstick skillet or griddle over medium heat. Once the butter is melted, scoop the batter into the pan in ¼-cup portions. Cook until small bubbles start to form and then pop on the pancakes, 1 to 2 minutes. Flip and continue to cook for an additional 2 to 3 minutes. Transfer to a plate and repeat with the remaining batter. You may need to wipe the pan clean with a paper towel and add more butter between batches.

To serve, top with sliced bananas and maple syrup.

Classic Eggs Benedict

This is a dish that Ed used to order from room service whenever we traveled as a family or with his band, Van Halen. He called it Eggy Benny, and I considered doing the same here but decided not to alter a classic. The dish is simple: poach the egg, crisp up some Canadian bacon, and make the hollandaise rich and creamy. Then indulge. Yes, indulge.

For the Hollandaise

1 stick (8 tablespoons) unsalted butter

1 tablespoon freshly squeezed lemon juice

3 large egg yolks

1 teaspoon Dijon mustard

Kosher salt

¼ teaspoon cayenne pepper

For Assembly

2 tablespoons distilled white vinegar

8 large eggs

Cooking spray

8 slices Canadian bacon

4 English muffins, split and lightly toasted

2 tablespoons chopped parsley, for garnish

Freshly ground black pepper

To make the hollandaise, melt the butter in a small saucepan over medium heat, then transfer it to a measuring cup.

Combine the lemon juice, egg yolks, mustard, ¼ teaspoon salt, and cayenne in a blender and blend on medium speed until lightened and smooth. With the motor running, very slowly add the melted butter. Increase the speed to high for a few seconds to thoroughly combine. Add a little bit of hot water to thin the sauce to a nice, spoonable consistency. Season to taste with salt. Keep in a warm place until ready to serve.

To poach the eggs, fill a wide, shallow pot with about 3 inches of water. Bring to a brisk simmer and add the vinegar. Crack 4 of the eggs into separate small bowls or ramekins, then gently slide the eggs into the water. Cook at a gentle simmer until the whites are set but the yolks are still runny, 2 to 3 minutes. Gently remove the eggs using a slotted spoon and place on a paper towel–lined plate to drain. Repeat with the remaining 4 eggs.

Meanwhile, heat a large nonstick skillet over medium-high heat. Once the pan is hot, add a thin layer of cooking spray. Add the Canadian bacon in an even layer. Cook until lightly browned, 2 minutes. Flip and cook until heated through, an additional minute or two.

To assemble, place the English muffins open-faced on a platter. Top each English muffin half with a piece of Canadian bacon and an egg. Drizzle the eggs with the hollandaise and garnish with parsley and pepper. Serve immediately.

Eggs in Purgatory with Kale

This dish is a variation of the Middle Eastern staple shakshuka, with an Italian twist. The culinary staff on Food Network's *Kids Baking Championship* introduced me to this dish, and now it's one of my favorite ways to enjoy eggs. It's especially great when my garden is overflowing with tomatoes, although using canned crushed tomatoes works just as well. The kale is for texture, vitamins, and because I love it.

2 tablespoons extra virgin olive oil

1 large shallot, halved and sliced

½ bunch lacinato kale, ribs removed, roughly chopped (3 to 4 cups)

Kosher salt and freshly ground black pepper

One 28-ounce can crushed tomatoes

½ cup roughly chopped jarred roasted red peppers

2 garlic cloves, grated

½ teaspoon Italian seasoning

1 tablespoon chopped oregano

2 tablespoons chopped basil, plus whole leaves for garnish

½ teaspoon Calabrian chili paste (optional)

4 large eggs

Freshly grated Parmesan, for garnish

Crusty bread, for serving

Heat the olive oil in a large straight-sided skillet over medium heat. Once the oil is shimmering, add the shallot. Cook, stirring occasionally, until it begins to soften, 2 to 3 minutes. Add the kale and season with a pinch of salt. Stir to combine. Cook until the kale is bright green and wilted, about 2 minutes.

Add the tomatoes, roasted red peppers, garlic, Italian seasoning, oregano, basil, Calabrian chili paste (if using), and ½ teaspoon salt to the pan. Stir to combine. Bring the mixture to a simmer, then reduce the heat to low and cook for 5 minutes so the flavors come together.

Use a wooden spoon to create four wells in the sauce. Crack an egg into a small bowl or measuring cup and gently tip it into one of the wells. Repeat with the remaining eggs. Season the eggs with a pinch of salt and pepper. Cover and cook on low until the whites are set but the yolks are still runny, 10 to 15 minutes.

Garnish with Parmesan and basil leaves. Serve with crusty bread.

Everyday Smoothie

This is just real food that makes my body feel real good. It powers me up for the day. I use frozen fruit in lieu of ice, and I save fresh fruit that I know I won't get to in the freezer.

1 cup frozen mixed berries
(strawberries, raspberries,
blackberries)

1 frozen banana

1 cup baby spinach

1 cup almond milk

Add the berries, banana, spinach, almond milk, and any add-ins to a high-powered blender. Blend on high speed until smooth.

Smoothie add-ins:

- Collagen powder
- Protein powder
- Greens powder
- Chia seeds
- Hemp hearts

- Turmeric
- Bee pollen
- Flaxseeds
- Spirulina
- Goji berries

Ham, Spinach, and Broccoli Omelet

One morning I was sitting in a hotel restaurant, enviously watching the chef make omelets at his very well-stocked omelet bar in the dining room. When I got back home, I used that for inspiration. I always have bacon or ham and broccoli and cheese in my fridge, but you can substitute all your favorites. I have listed a bunch of mine.

2 large eggs

¼ cup chopped ham

Kosher salt and freshly ground black pepper

1 tablespoon unsalted butter

¼ cup freshly grated sharp Cheddar (about 1 ounce)

¼ cup roughly chopped spinach

¼ cup roughly chopped blanched broccoli

Whisk the eggs in a medium bowl, then add the ham and stir to combine. Season the mixture with ½ teaspoon salt and a pinch of pepper.

Melt the butter in a small nonstick skillet over medium heat. Add the egg and ham mixture and use a silicone spatula to push the edges of the egg mixture toward the center, so the uncooked eggs come in contact with the hot pan. Continue lifting the eggs and tilting the pan until the eggs are almost set. Sprinkle with the cheese and spinach. Add the broccoli to one side of the omelet. Using the spatula, carefully fold half of the omelet over to close it like a book. Gently slide the omelet from the pan to a plate. Serve immediately.

Cook's Note

Omelets are a great way to use up whatever you have in the fridge. You can substitute the ingredients in this omelet with any of these options:

- Bacon
- Breakfast sausage
- Italian sausage
- Prosciutto
- American cheese
- Swiss cheese
- Goat cheese
- Feta
- Chopped bell peppers

- Leftover grilled vegetables (peppers, zucchini, eggplant, onions)
- Roasted sweet potato
- Sautéed mushrooms
- Fresh herbs
- Quartered cherry tomatoes
- Caramelized onions

Maple Pecan Scones

Many years ago, my dear friend Jane Leeves raved about a delectable pastry she had tasted at Starbucks—the maple scone. This was in the early 1990s, before there was a Starbucks on every corner and before we worked together on the TV series *Hot in Cleveland*. "Oh, my dear, they're absolutely divine," she exclaimed. "You must give them a try." I did, and she was right. The maple sweetness and pecan crunch, paired with my morning coffee, is a delightful way to start the day.

For the Scones

2 tablespoons maple syrup

⅓ cup heavy cream, plus more for brushing

1 large egg

1 teaspoon vanilla extract

1½ cups all-purpose flour, plus more for dusting

½ cup oat flour

¼ cup granulated sugar

1 tablespoon baking powder

¼ teaspoon kosher salt

6 tablespoons cold unsalted butter, cut into ½-inch cubes and kept in the freezer until ready to use

½ cup chopped pecans

For the Glaze

1½ cups powdered sugar

¼ cup milk (2% or whole)

½ teaspoon maple extract

½ cup chopped pecans

Preheat the oven to 400°F. Line a baking sheet with parchment paper.

To make the scones, whisk together the maple syrup, cream, egg, and vanilla in a small bowl.

In a large bowl, whisk together the all-purpose flour, oat flour, sugar, baking powder, and salt. Add the cold cubed butter and use a pastry cutter or a fork to cut the butter into the dry ingredients until you have pea-size pieces. Add the wet ingredients and mix until just combined. Add the pecans and mix until incorporated.

Turn the dough out onto a lightly floured surface. Working quickly to keep the butter cold, knead any loose flour to form a cohesive dough. Form the dough into an 8-inch circle, then cut it into eight equal triangles. Use a spatula to transfer the scones to the prepared baking sheet and brush the tops with cream. Bake for 15 to 18 minutes, until lightly golden brown.

Let cool for 5 minutes on the baking sheet before transferring them to a wire rack to cool completely.

To make the glaze, whisk together the powdered sugar, milk, and maple extract in a medium bowl until smooth. Spoon over the cooled scones. Top with the pecans. Let the glazed scones set for about 15 minutes before serving.

Wolfie's Egg Bites

My son has spent much of the past three years on tour with his band, Mammoth (in fact, as I write this, I am a day away from flying to Paris to see him perform there), and he frequently pops into Starbucks for breakfast because he likes their egg bites. I re-created them here for him, his wife, and anyone else who wants to enjoy a quick, tasty breakfast before hitting the road in the morning. (Wolfie, these are for you. With love, Ma.)

4 slices bacon, finely diced

6 large eggs

⅔ cup low-fat cottage cheese

⅔ cup freshly grated Gruyère (about 2½ ounces)

¾ teaspoon kosher salt

¼ teaspoon freshly ground black pepper

Cooking spray

Special equipment

2 silicone egg molds with covers, pressure cooker

Place the bacon in a medium nonstick skillet and cook over medium-high heat until the fat has rendered and the bacon is crisp, 3 to 4 minutes. Use a slotted spoon to transfer it to a paper towel–lined plate to cool slightly.

Combine the eggs, cottage cheese, Gruyère, salt, and pepper in a blender. Start blending on low speed, gradually increasing the speed to high, until the mixture is completely smooth, about 10 seconds.

Lightly spray your silicone molds with cooking spray. Place 1 cup of water in the base of the pressure cooker.

Evenly divide the egg mixture between the prepared molds. Sprinkle the bacon evenly among the cups and use a spoon to help submerge the bacon. Cover the molds with the silicone cover and transfer to the pressure cooker.

Cook on high pressure according to the manufacturer's instructions for 10 minutes. Let the pressure release naturally for 10 minutes. Manually release any remaining pressure, then carefully remove the lid and use oven mitts to remove the molds.

While the egg bites are still hot, use an offset spatula to loosen them from the molds and invert onto a plate. Serve warm or at room temperature. Store in an airtight container in the fridge for up to 1 week. To reheat, microwave for 20 to 30 seconds.

A Good Day for a Sandwich

Sometimes I just crave a good sandwich. I don't know what is going on between my brain and body when that happens, but I will obsess about two slices of bread and what I can put between them. I not only taste them, I see them. Turkey. Ham and cheese. A BLT. Egg salad. It's a Sandwich Hall of Fame. Like the Rock and Roll Hall of Fame in Cleveland, I'm talking nothing but classics. Like hearing Elton John's "Tiny Dancer" takes me back to junior high, one bite of a fresh ham and cheese on a baguette and I'm sitting at a café in Paris.

On the day I started work on this cookbook, a friend came over for lunch and I made a trio of tea sandwiches. I had such a good time preparing the fillings, trimming the crust, slicing each sandwich into quarters, and placing them on a beautiful dish. I flashed back to the first time I was in London and indulged in a formal tea at a fancy hotel. It's amazing how that happens. My mother made me a bologna sandwich—soft white bread, a generous slather of mayo, and a slice of Oscar Mayer's finest—for lunch almost every day of elementary school, and to this day it remains one of my most delicious food memories ever.

I have spent years thinking about the reasons for this, eager to apply that same time-traveling magic to other dishes, and I have come to realize it's more than the ingredients. I mean there's nothing magical about bologna and mayo. Well, on second thought . . . But seriously, it has to do with the connection to my mother and me. It was the intent she put into making those sandwiches. I know this sounds cliché, but it was the love that went into that daily bologna sandwich. When I opened my brown paper lunch bag, I felt her presence. She was with me. She was taking care of me.

When I was pregnant with my son, I was hungry, really hungry—finally, I didn't feel like I had to count calories or watch what I ate—and my mom brought me delicious Italian sub sandwiches, which I devoured. She enjoyed driving them over to the house where Ed and I lived and, after I gave birth, she continued her much-appreciated delivery service, playing with Wolfie while I savored every layered bite of salami, capicola, ham, and cheese. Again, she was being a mom and taking care of her family, expressing her love by showing up, giving me a hug, and putting this aptly named "hero" sandwich on a plate with a simple directive—eat!

This is what cooking is all about—sharing the warmth and joy and love in my heart with those who matter most to me. A tasty sandwich can be simple or packed full of nuance, but it gets right to the point I want to make in this book. You must be thoughtful and intentional to make a good one.

A few years ago, my friend Jenn Harris wrote a story for the *Los Angeles Times* about a man named Rosario Mazzeo who owns an Italian deli in Pasadena, California. He has made an Italian sandwich for so long that he is known simply as "the Sandwich Man." It started in 1959 when his wine supplier asked for something to eat, and he made his first sandwich: a fresh Italian roll, slices of capicola, mortadella, salami, and provolone, and a generous splash of olive oil. The next day, the wine supplier brought in five coworkers. Seven decades later, his tiny Roma Market makes six hundred of the exact same sandwiches every day—more on weekends. His secret? Using the best ingredients. And caring about the quality.

I realize these are life lessons, not just cooking tips, and that's fine with me. As far as I'm concerned, a good cookbook is a collection of life lessons, the kinds of lessons we should embrace and indulge in. Back when I was pregnant, if I didn't have one of my mother's subs, I would drive to my neighborhood deli for a thick turkey and roast beef sandwich on rye with Muenster cheese and lots of mayo and mustard. After a couple of months, I only had to walk through the door and my sandwich would be waiting for me. The guys behind the counter loved seeing me because I was their biggest fan.

It's been over thirty years since I ordered that sandwich, but one chilly January afternoon I craved something delicious for lunch. I thought back to how happy I was when I was pregnant with Wolfie, and suddenly I was thinking about that deli sandwich. My mouth started to water, so I made one for myself. Except my version was half the size and I added hot cherry peppers because, well, I love hot cherry peppers. And one bite later, I was in heaven. I declared it a good day for a sandwich.

Ultimately, that's the lasting takeaway about a good sandwich: happiness—yours or someone else's—is in your own hands.

Ham and Brie
Sandwiches on
Pretzel Buns

(page 36)

SANDWICHES

"Sandwiches are traditionally eaten at lunch, but I encourage you to try any of these delicious sandwiches for dinner."

1970s Special Turkey Sandwich

Back in the 1970s, the local health food store was the place to buy your peanut butter, carob, and sunflower seeds. Sandwiches all came on wheat bread with a thick layer of alfalfa sprouts. I'm pushing for a comeback with this turkey sandwich. It's all about the sprouts, though I tend to prefer broccoli sprouts. I love the crunch—and my memories of bell bottoms and puka shells.

4 slices Multigrain Seeded
    Bread (page 126 or
    store-bought)

2 slices Havarti

3 tablespoons Roasted Garlic
    Mayo (page 315 or store-
    bought mayo)

8 ounces thinly sliced
    deli turkey

1 vine-ripened tomato, sliced

Kosher salt and freshly
    ground black pepper

1 cup broccoli or
    alfalfa sprouts

Arrange the bread on a clean work surface. Place a slice of cheese on both of the bottom slices of bread. Spread the mayo evenly on the top pieces of bread. Evenly divide the turkey on top of the cheese. Place the tomato slices on top of the turkey and season with salt and pepper. Top the tomato with the sprouts and the top piece of bread. Slice on the diagonal and serve.

Cuban Sandwich with Slow-Cooker Pulled Pork

I had a Cuban sandwich for the first time in Miami when I visited Wolfie, who was there working with friends. It was love at first bite, and I never forgot that celebration of flavors. This is my variation on the classic.

3 pounds boneless pork shoulder

½ teaspoon ground cumin

3 garlic cloves, finely chopped

Kosher salt and freshly ground black pepper

3 tablespoons freshly squeezed orange juice

1 tablespoon freshly squeezed lime juice

Four 6-inch soft sub loaves, split

About 3 tablespoons mayonnaise

About 3 tablespoons yellow mustard

4 ounces thinly sliced ham

6 ounces sliced Swiss cheese

1 cup dill pickle chips

About 2 tablespoons unsalted butter

Rub the pork all over with the cumin, garlic, 1½ teaspoons salt, and ¼ teaspoon pepper. Place in a slow cooker and drizzle with the orange and lime juices. Cook on high until the meat is tender and falling apart, about 6 hours. Transfer to a cutting board and coarsely shred with two forks.

Spread half of each sub loaf with mayo and the other with mustard. Build the sandwiches with the pulled pork, ham, Swiss, and pickles (you will have some pork left over).

Melt 1 tablespoon of the butter in a large skillet over medium heat. Place two of the sandwiches in the skillet and cover with another skillet, weighing it down with a heavy can or pot. Cook until golden brown, about 4 minutes. Flip the sandwiches, replace the top skillet and weight, and continue to cook until the other side is golden brown and the cheese is melted, about 3 minutes more. Repeat with the remaining sandwiches and butter. Store any leftover pork in an airtight container. It will keep for 5 days in the refrigerator or even 6 months in the freezer. The leftovers can be used for nachos, tacos, burritos, cottage pie, or eggrolls—the possibilities are mouthwateringly endless!

Egg Salad Sandwich

I love a good egg salad sandwich, but I hate peeling eggs. Then I saw a hack on TikTok that showed a way to "hard-boil" eggs in the oven, and I had to share it here. Essentially you are baking eggs in a water bath. They taste great, and so does this sandwich. Maybe I'm the last one to know this trick, but life is better now that I do.

Cooking spray

8 large eggs

¼ cup mayonnaise

2 teaspoons Dijon mustard

¼ teaspoon onion powder

1 tablespoon chopped dill

1 tablespoon chopped chives

Kosher salt and freshly
  ground black pepper

8 slices Milk Bread
  (page 128 or a thick-sliced
  store-bought white
  bread), toasted

Preheat the oven to 350°F. Spray a 9 × 5-inch loaf pan with cooking spray.

Crack the eggs into the prepared loaf pan. Create a water bath by placing the loaf pan in a 9 × 13-inch baking dish. Fill the baking dish two-thirds full with cold water. Transfer the baking dish to the oven and bake for 30 to 35 minutes, until the whites are completely set and the yolks have a "hard-boiled" consistency.

Let sit for 5 minutes before using a butter knife or an offset spatula to loosen the eggs from the sides of the pan. Use a spatula to transfer the eggs to a cutting board and chop finely. Add the chopped eggs to a medium bowl along with the mayo, mustard, onion powder, dill, and chives and stir to combine. Season to taste with salt and pepper.

To assemble the sandwiches, divide the mixture evenly among four slices of the bread, then top each sandwich with the remaining bread. Slice on the diagonal and serve.

Garlic Confit BLT

I wanted to do something with garlic confit, which I love, so I created this sandwich especially for this book. Its sweet, caramelized taste with the savory bacon and creamy avocado is a truly memorable first, second, and third bite. I can't wait for you to try it.

6 slices thick-cut bacon

4 slices white sandwich bread, toasted

2 tablespoons mayonnaise

8 confit garlic cloves (page 319)

½ avocado, sliced

Kosher salt and freshly ground black pepper

1 heirloom tomato, sliced

4 leaves green-leaf lettuce

Preheat the oven to 400°F. Line a baking sheet with foil.

Place the bacon on the prepared baking sheet and bake for 15 to 20 minutes, until crisp. Transfer the bacon to a paper towel–lined plate to drain. Set aside.

To assemble the sandwiches, arrange the toast on a clean work surface. Spread the mayo evenly on the two bottom pieces of toast. Divide the garlic confit evenly between the top two pieces of toast and use a butter knife to spread the garlic on the toast. Lay a few slices of avocado on top of the garlic and season with salt and pepper.

On each piece of toast with mayo, layer three pieces of bacon, then top with a few slices of tomato. Season the tomato with salt and pepper. Top with the lettuce and place the piece of toast with the avocado on top. Press down to sandwich everything together. Slice on the diagonal and serve.

Ham and Brie Sandwiches on Pretzel Buns

This sandwich reminds me of my trip to Paris when I was shooting the opening credits for my TV series *Café Americain*. During the shoot, one of the crew members went around the corner and picked up a few ham and brie sandwiches on pretzel baguettes. I never forgot them, and this simple sandwich is *toujours délicieux*.

PHOTO ON PAGE 26

8 Pretzel Buns (page 130 or store-bought)

1 stick (8 tablespoons) unsalted butter, room temperature

2 tablespoons Dijon mustard

1 pound thinly sliced French ham

6 ounces Brie, sliced

2 cups arugula

Preheat the oven to 350°F. Line a baking sheet with parchment paper.

Place the pretzel buns on the prepared baking sheet and transfer to the oven for 10 minutes, until warm.

Let the buns sit until they are just cool enough to handle, then slice in half.

Spread the softened butter on each of the cut sides of the buns, using about 1 tablespoon per bun. Spread mustard on the bottom half of each bun.

Delicately fold and layer the ham on top of the mustard. Top with the Brie and about ¼ cup of arugula. Sandwich with the top buns. Serve immediately.

" A good recipe is like a successful relationship.

It starts with a feeling in your gut and a tingle on your tongue.

It requires optimism, taking chances, forgiving mistakes, and perseverance.

And it ends with love. "

Mom's Hero

Anyone who has read my books and heard me interviewed over the years knows that I craved my mom's Italian sub sandwich while I was pregnant with my son. Maybe one day I'll be making these for my daughter-in-law . . . hint, hint.

2 heaping cups shredded iceberg lettuce

½ cup diced red onion

½ cup chopped pepperoncini peppers

⅓ cup Creamy Italian Dressing (page 321)

Four 6-inch ciabatta rolls

8 slices provolone

4 ounces thinly sliced Black Forest ham

4 ounces thinly sliced capicola (preferably hot)

4 ounces thinly sliced Genoa salami

2 vine-ripened tomatoes, very thinly sliced and seasoned with kosher salt and freshly ground pepper

¼ cup thinly sliced basil

Toss the iceberg, onion, and pepperoncini with 2 tablespoons of the Italian dressing in a medium bowl.

Using a serrated knife, slice open the rolls. Drizzle 2 teaspoons of the dressing on the bottom of each roll and spread evenly. Place two slices of provolone on the dressing, then evenly divide the cold cuts, tomatoes, and lettuce mixture evenly among the bottom rolls. Top with the basil. Drizzle the remaining dressing on the top halves of the rolls and place on top to make sandwiches. Wrap in wax paper. Slice in half and serve.

Peanut Butter, Banana, and Honey Sandwich

Just because you're an adult doesn't mean you can't still indulge in this childhood favorite. I won't judge if you want to buy all the ingredients at the store. For me, however, the point is making this from scratch and then listening to everyone talk about the foods they loved as kids.

2 slices Milk Bread (page 128 or store-bought sliced white bread)

2 tablespoons Homemade Peanut Butter (page 310 or store-bought)

½ large banana, sliced

1 teaspoon Turmeric Ginger Honey (page 311 or store-bought honey)

Arrange the bread on a clean work surface. Spread 1 tablespoon of peanut butter on each piece of bread. Shingle the sliced banana on the bottom piece of bread and drizzle the honey on top. Sandwich the two slices together and press gently to adhere. Slice in half and serve.

Spinach Ricotta Grilled Cheese

There is really no limit to what you can do with a grilled cheese sandwich. I will add chutney or honey, or go with thin tomato slices, depending on the way I feel. Lately, spinach and ricotta along with the richness of a good Parmigiano-Reggiano has been my favorite way to amp up this classic. It tastes like I'm doing something special.

1 tablespoon extra virgin olive oil

5 ounces baby spinach

Kosher salt and freshly ground black pepper

½ cup ricotta

1 cup freshly grated mozzarella (about 4 ounces)

½ cup freshly grated Parmigiano-Reggiano (about 2 ounces)

8 slices Milk Bread (page 128 or any sturdy bread), sliced ⅓ inch thick

½ stick (4 tablespoons) unsalted butter, room temperature

Heat a large skillet over medium-high heat. Add the olive oil, spinach, and a scant ½ teaspoon salt. Sauté until the spinach has completely wilted, about 3 to 5 minutes. Transfer the spinach to a strainer set over a bowl and let cool. When the spinach is cool enough to handle, squeeze out as much liquid as possible. Wipe the skillet and set aside to toast sandwiches later.

Roughly chop the spinach and add it to a medium bowl along with the ricotta, mozzarella, Parmigiano-Reggiano, ¼ teaspoon salt, and ¼ teaspoon pepper. Stir to combine.

Arrange the bread on a clean work surface. Spread each slice with 1½ teaspoons of the butter. Heat the skillet over medium heat. Lay four of the slices in the skillet, butter side down. Scoop about ⅓ cup of the ricotta mixture onto each slice. Spread the mixture evenly to cover the whole slice, then top with the other slices of bread, butter side up. Cook until the first side is golden and toasted, 2 to 3 minutes. Carefully flip the sandwiches and cook until the other side is toasted and the cheese is melty, an additional 2 to 3 minutes.

Transfer the sandwiches to a clean work surface and let them cool for 1 minute before slicing.

A Trio of Tea Sandwiches

The last time I was in London, I indulged in a delightful high tea at my hotel. One of the highlights was the exquisite assortment of bite-size sandwiches that accompanied the tea service. Impressed, I decided to re-create them at home when I hosted friends for lunch. The bite-size sandwiches added an elegant and playful element to the meal and showed that I wanted to make our get-together extra special.

Smoked Salmon

4 slices white bread

4 ounces whipped
   cream cheese

2 radishes, thinly sliced

2 ounces smoked salmon

Arrange the bread on a clean work surface. Spread the cream cheese on all four pieces of bread. Divide the radishes between the bottom pieces of bread. Arrange the smoked salmon on the top pieces of bread. Sandwich the tops and bottoms together and press lightly to adhere. Use a serrated knife to cut the crusts off the sandwiches. Cut into triangles and arrange on a serving platter.

Cucumber

4 ounces whipped
   cream cheese

2 tablespoons
   chopped chives

4 slices Multigrain Seeded
   Bread (page 126 or
   store-bought)

¼ English cucumber, peeled
   and thinly sliced

Freshly ground black pepper

Mix together the cream cheese and chives in a small bowl. Arrange the bread on a clean work surface. Spread the chive cream cheese on all four pieces of bread. Shingle the cucumber on the bottom pieces of bread. Season with a pinch of pepper. Sandwich the tops and bottoms together and press lightly to adhere. Use a serrated knife to cut the crusts off the sandwiches. Cut each sandwich into three rectangles and arrange on a serving platter.

Ham and Cheese

4 slices Multigrain Cinnamon
   Raisin Bread (page 120 or
   store-bought)

3 tablespoons salted butter,
   room temperature

4 ounces Gruyère,
   thinly sliced

4 thin slices Black Forest ham

Arrange the bread on a clean work surface. Spread the butter on all four pieces of bread. Divide the cheese between the bottom pieces of bread. Arrange the ham on the top pieces of bread. Sandwich the tops and bottoms together and press lightly to adhere. Use a serrated knife to cut the crusts off the sandwiches. Cut into triangles or rectangles and arrange on a serving platter.

Tuna Salad Sandwich

Everyone needs a classic tuna salad sandwich in their repertoire, and this one fits the bill. You can play with the herbs to your individual preference. I like tuna packed in oil for the additional flavor, but I know others are devoted to the water-packed alternative.

One 6- to 7-ounce jar olive oil–packed tuna, drained

1 celery stalk, finely chopped (about ¼ cup)

½ small shallot, finely chopped (about 2 tablespoons)

2 tablespoons chopped parsley

1 teaspoon chopped tarragon

2 tablespoons mayonnaise

1 teaspoon Dijon mustard

1 tablespoon freshly squeezed lemon juice

4 slices Milk Bread (page 128 or a thick-sliced store-bought white bread), toasted

1 vine-ripened tomato, sliced

Kosher salt and freshly ground black pepper

Place the tuna in a medium bowl and use two forks to flake it into smaller pieces. Add the celery, shallot, parsley, and tarragon and mix to combine.

Whisk together the mayo, mustard, and lemon juice in a small bowl until smooth. Add the mayo mixture to the tuna and mix until evenly combined. Season to taste with salt and pepper.

To assemble the sandwiches, arrange the toast on a clean work surface. Divide the tuna salad evenly among all four pieces of bread, spreading it to coat the entire slice. Place a few slices of tomato on two pieces of the bread. Season the tomato with salt and pepper and place the other two pieces of bread on top of the tomato, tuna side down. Slice on the diagonal and serve.

Refrigerator
Pickled
Vegetables
(page 57)

SNACKS & APPS

"Some of my favorite meals consist entirely of appetizers. A variety of deliciousness on small plates. And it always seems like a party."

Bacon-Wrapped Jalapeño Poppers

Deep-fried jalapeño poppers sent me to Jenny Craig years ago, but I was eating them for all the wrong reasons. In fact, I don't think I ever "tasted" a single one. So, including this recipe is a personal victory of sorts, in addition to being wildly delicious. I'm indulging in it. You should, too.

4 ounces cream cheese, room temperature

½ cup freshly grated smoked Gouda (about 2 ounces)

½ cup freshly grated mild Cheddar (about 2 ounces)

2 teaspoons finely chopped chives

1 teaspoon lime zest

1½ teaspoons freshly squeezed lime juice

¼ teaspoon kosher salt

Freshly ground black pepper

8 jalapeños, halved lengthwise, seeds removed

8 slices bacon, halved crosswise

Preheat the oven to 425°F. Line a baking sheet with foil.

Mix together the cream cheese, Gouda, Cheddar, chives, lime zest and juice, salt, and a pinch of pepper in a medium bowl until evenly combined.

Divide the cream cheese mixture among the jalapeño halves, pressing to fill all the way to the top edge.

Wrap a slice of bacon around each stuffed jalapeño so the ends of the bacon lie underneath. Place the wrapped jalapeños, stuffed side up, on the prepared baking sheet. Bake for 16 to 18 minutes, until the bacon is crispy and the cheese mixture is just beginning to bubble out from the top and bottom of the jalapeños. Let cool 10 minutes before serving.

Bagna Cauda and Crudités

Bagna cauda (roughly translated as "hot bath") is an intensely flavored Italian dip. You can dip veggies, crusty bread, or a sturdy cabbage leaf in it, or spread it on pizza dough instead of red sauce—it all works as a vehicle to get this deliciousness into your mouth.

One 2-ounce tin anchovies
  packed in olive oil

8 garlic cloves,
  roughly chopped

⅔ cup extra virgin olive oil

5 tablespoons unsalted
  butter, cubed

Crusty bread, for serving

Assorted vegetables, such
  as raw cabbage, celery,
  blanched asparagus,
  endive, fennel, zucchini,
  or radishes, for serving

Combine the entire tin of anchovies (including the oil), garlic, and olive oil in a small food processor. Blend until everything is finely chopped and evenly combined.

Transfer the anchovy mixture to a small saucepan and add the butter. Cook over medium heat, stirring frequently, until the butter is melted and the mixture is simmering gently. Reduce the heat to the very lowest setting and cook, stirring occasionally, until the garlic flavor has mellowed, about 15 minutes. The sauce will separate; this is normal.

Remove from the heat and let sit for 5 minutes before serving. Serve with crusty bread and assorted vegetables.

Spring Radishes
with Tzatziki
(page 56)

Roasted
Antipasto with
Crostini
(page 64)

Classic
Hummus
(page 60)

Bagna Cauda
and Crudités
(opposite)

Zesty Cheddar
Cheese Crackers
(page 65)

Baguette Snacks

File this under "Easy, Delicious Ideas." It's not so much a recipe as it is a prompt (or aide-mémoire) for when you need an idea. Anything works on top of a halved baguette—white bean puree, peanut butter and honey, cheese and tomato. You're just putting delicious ingredients on toast.

Caprese Baguette

¼ baguette, sliced in half lengthwise

Extra virgin olive oil

1 vine-ripened tomato, sliced

⅓ cup ciliegine mozzarella balls, halved

Kosher salt and freshly ground black pepper

4 slices prosciutto

Basil leaves, for garnish

Preheat the oven to 450°F. Line a baking sheet with parchment paper.

Place the baguette halves cut side up on the prepared baking sheet. Drizzle with olive oil. Top with the tomato and mozzarella and season with salt and pepper. Transfer to the oven and bake for 10 to 15 minutes, until the cheese is melted.

Remove from the oven and top with the prosciutto and basil. Serve immediately.

Ham and Butter Baguette

¼ baguette, sliced in half lengthwise

2 tablespoons European-style salted butter

4 thin slices prosciutto cotto

4 cornichons, halved lengthwise

Freshly ground black pepper

Spread a tablespoon of butter on each half of the baguette. Top with prosciutto cotto, cornichons, and pepper.

Tapenade and Roasted Red Pepper Baguette

¼ baguette, sliced in half
　　lengthwise

Extra virgin olive oil

¼ cup Tapenade (page 334
　　or store-bought)

4 slices Calabrese salami

¼ cup sliced roasted
　　red pepper

Preheat the oven to broil. Place the baguette halves cut side up on a baking sheet. Drizzle with olive oil. Transfer the baguette to the oven and broil until the bread is lightly crisp, 1 to 2 minutes.

Spread the tapenade on the toasted baguette and top with salami and roasted red pepper.

Prep time: 10 minutes　　　*Serves* 4

PHOTO
ON PAGE
53

Spring Radishes with Tzatziki

Spring is the season for love and radishes and people like me who love radishes. I have been known to serve radishes simply with butter and salt, as they do in France, but I also enjoy this version and especially the way radishes plate on top of a layer of tzatziki. The crisp, fresh taste lives up to the beauty of this presentation. Use more tzatziki if you like a thicker base.

1 to 1½ cups Easy Tzatziki
　　(page 334 or store-bought)

1 bunch multicolor radishes,
　　trimmed and halved

1 small watermelon radish,
　　trimmed, halved, and sliced

1 lemon

¼ cup mint leaves

2 tablespoons dill fronds

Flaky sea salt

Freshly ground black pepper

Extra virgin olive oil

Spread the tzatziki in an even, thin layer on a plate or small serving platter. Arrange the radishes on top of the tzatziki.

Use a fine zester to zest half of the lemon over the radishes and tzatziki. Top with mint leaves, dill fronds, flaky salt, pepper, and a drizzle of olive oil. Serve immediately.

Refrigerator Pickled Vegetables

I want you to discover how easy it is to make your own delicious pickled vegetables. They make the best snacks and serve as an impressive addition to any type of charcuterie board or antipasto plate. For full flavor, I recommend refrigerating the pickles for at least 24 hours before nibbling. This recipe works for standard cucumber refrigerator pickles as well as any other assortment you choose.

¾ cup distilled white vinegar

1 heaping teaspoon sugar

1 heaping teaspoon
   kosher salt

2 garlic cloves, smashed

1 teaspoon black peppercorns

1 teaspoon yellow
   mustard seeds

½ teaspoon red pepper flakes

2 bay leaves

Combine 1¼ cups water, the vinegar, sugar, salt, garlic, peppercorns, mustard seeds, pepper flakes, and bay leaves in a small saucepan. Heat the mixture over medium heat until the salt and sugar are dissolved. Remove from the heat. Add your desired vegetable to a quart jar or container and pour the hot pickling mixture over the vegetables, covering it completely. Let cool to room temperature, cover, and refrigerate. Let sit in the fridge for at least 24 hours before enjoying. This recipe can easily be doubled or tripled to make large batches of pickles.

Cook's Note

This recipe can be used for a variety of vegetables, such as:

- Cucumbers (sliced into chips or spears)
- Red onion (halved and thinly sliced)
- Cauliflower (cut into small florets)
- Mushrooms (wash and boil mushrooms for 15 minutes first, then drain and add pickling liquid)
- Okra
- Green beans
- Carrots (sliced into coins)
- Jalapeños (sliced into coins)
- Garlic (omit the garlic from the pickling recipe)
- Radishes (sliced)
- Zucchini (sliced into coins or spears)
- Fennel (thinly sliced)
- Bell peppers or mini bell peppers (sliced)
- Asparagus
- Beets (peel and boil beets first, or use canned beets)

Feel free to get creative and add some extra flavor to your pickle brine with:

- Herb sprigs (dill, parsley, chives, cilantro)
- Citrus peel (lemon, lime, grapefruit, orange)
- Cardamom pods
- Coriander seeds
- Cumin seeds
- Fennel seeds
- Caraway seeds

Clams Casino

This is my childhood in a clamshell, and though they say you can't go back in time, I do— and I take bacon, shallots, and red bell pepper with me. Dice everything as finely as possible so it will fit snugly in the clam shells.

24 to 26 littleneck clams

½ cup dry white wine

3 slices center-cut bacon, cut into ¼-inch dice

½ cup finely diced shallot (2 to 3 shallots)

¼ cup finely diced red bell pepper

3 garlic cloves, grated

½ cup panko bread crumbs

2 tablespoons extra virgin olive oil

Kosher salt and freshly ground black pepper

1 tablespoon chopped chives, for garnish

Soak the clams in cold water to purge any sand or impurities, about 20 minutes. Scrub them to remove any dirt or barnacles from the outer shells. Drain the clams.

Combine the wine and cleaned clams in a large saucepan, cover, and cook over medium heat. After a few minutes, check to see if any of the clams have opened. Once they start opening, transfer the open clams to a large bowl to cool. Cover and wait another minute or so before checking to see if any more have opened. Discard any clams that don't open. Once all the clams have been removed, reduce the heat to low and let the wine and clam juice mixture reduce until there is ⅓ cup of liquid left.

Meanwhile, heat a large skillet over medium heat. Add the bacon and cook, stirring occasionally, until the fat begins to render and the bacon browns slightly, about 2 minutes. Add the shallot and red pepper to the pan and cook until slightly softened, 2 to 3 minutes. Add the garlic and stir to combine. Cook until the garlic is evenly incorporated and fragrant, about 1 minute. Use a fine-mesh strainer to strain the reduced wine and clam juice mixture into the pan. Stir to combine and cook until the mixture is cohesive, about 2 minutes. Remove from the heat and let cool slightly.

Preheat the oven to broil. Line a baking pan with foil.

Mix the panko, olive oil, ¼ teaspoon salt, and ¼ teaspoon pepper together in a small bowl. Set aside.

Carefully remove the top shell from each of the clams and use a spoon to loosen the meat from the bottom shell. Place the meat back into the bottom shell and then onto the prepared baking pan.

Divide the bacon mixture evenly among the clams, using a spoon to pack the mixture tightly into the shell. Top each clam with about 1 teaspoon of the panko mixture.

Transfer the clams to the broiler and broil for 30 seconds to 1 minute, just until the bread crumbs are golden brown. Keep an eye on them as the browning can happen quite quickly.

Remove from the oven and use tongs to transfer the clams to a serving plate. Garnish with chives. Serve immediately.

Classic Hummus

PHOTO ON PAGE 53

I like having good, zesty hummus in the fridge for dipping raw vegetables or pita chips. The food processor does all the work. Play with the amounts of cumin, lemon juice, and garlic salt to adjust the flavor to your liking. The crispy chickpeas add a fun crunch.

Two 15-ounce cans
   chickpeas, drained
   and rinsed

½ teaspoon baking soda

¼ cup tahini

1 teaspoon ground cumin

1 garlic clove, grated

⅓ cup freshly squeezed lemon
   juice (from 2 to 3 lemons)

Kosher salt

¼ cup extra virgin olive oil,
   plus more for garnish

Paprika, for garnish

Chopped parsley, for garnish

Crispy Chickpeas (recipe
   follows), for garnish

Pita chips and assorted
   crudités, for serving

Combine the chickpeas and baking soda in a medium saucepan with enough water to cover by 1 inch. Bring the mixture to a boil over medium-high heat, then reduce the heat and simmer for 20 minutes. The chickpeas will be very soft. (Boiling the chickpeas with baking soda will help break down the outer layer of the chickpeas and make the hummus smooth.)

Drain the chickpeas well and transfer to a food processor, along with the tahini, cumin, garlic, lemon juice, and 1 teaspoon salt. Blend until the mixture is completely smooth and silky, 2 to 3 minutes. With the machine running, slowly stream in the olive oil and blend until incorporated. Season to taste with more salt.

Transfer the hummus to a shallow bowl and smooth it out to create a flat surface. Garnish with olive oil, a sprinkle of paprika, chopped parsley, and crispy chickpeas. Serve with pita chips and crudités. Store leftovers in an airtight container in the fridge for up to 1 week.

Crispy Chickpeas

If you don't already keep crispy chickpeas handy, you will. When the munchies hit, grab a handful of these. They're also great to toss in a salad.

Two 15-ounce cans chickpeas, drained, rinsed, and thoroughly dried with paper towels

3 tablespoons extra virgin olive oil

1 teaspoon garlic powder

1 teaspoon onion powder

1 teaspoon smoked paprika

1 teaspoon ground cumin

½ teaspoon chili powder

½ teaspoon chipotle powder

1 teaspoon kosher salt

½ teaspoon freshly ground black pepper

Preheat the oven to 375°F. Line a baking sheet with parchment paper.

Mix together the chickpeas and olive oil in a large bowl. Add the garlic powder, onion powder, smoked paprika, cumin, chili powder, chipotle powder, salt, and pepper and toss to coat the chickpeas in the seasoning.

Transfer the seasoned chickpeas to the prepared baking sheet, spreading them out in an even layer. Bake for 35 to 40 minutes, tossing after 20 minutes, until the chickpeas are golden brown and crispy. Let cool for 5 minutes before serving.

Store in an airtight container at room temperature for up to 1 week.

Oven-"Fried" Okra

I love the taste of fried foods, but I hate bringing out the oil and the mess that I must clean up afterward. Instead, I fake fry my okra in the oven and serve it with a really great dipping sauce, like the one here or my Jalapeño Ranch Dressing (page 320). Serve this as snacks for the family or bring out a platter for company. It'll be gobbled up.

For the Dipping Sauce

¼ cup mayonnaise

¼ cup sour cream

2 teaspoons Cajun seasoning

½ teaspoon lemon zest

1 tablespoon freshly squeezed
   lemon juice

Kosher salt and freshly
   ground black pepper

For the Okra

1½ cups buttermilk

1 pound okra, trimmed and
   cut into ½-inch pieces

1 cup cornmeal

½ cup all-purpose flour

2 teaspoons Cajun seasoning

½ teaspoon onion powder

½ teaspoon garlic powder

½ teaspoon kosher salt

Cooking spray

Preheat the oven to 400°F. Line a baking sheet with parchment paper.

To make the dipping sauce, combine the mayo, sour cream, Cajun seasoning, and lemon zest and juice in a small bowl. Season to taste with salt and pepper. Cover and store in the fridge until ready to serve.

To make the okra, pour the buttermilk into a large bowl. Add the sliced okra and stir to coat the pieces completely in the buttermilk. In a medium bowl, stir together the cornmeal, flour, Cajun seasoning, onion powder, garlic powder, and salt.

Working with a few pieces of okra at a time, transfer them to the bowl with the cornmeal mixture and toss gently to completely coat them. Shake off any excess coating, then place on the prepared baking sheet. Repeat with the remaining okra. Once all the okra is on the baking sheet, liberally spray it with cooking spray.

Bake for 25 to 30 minutes, flipping halfway through, until the okra is crisp and golden brown in places.

Let cool for a few minutes before serving with the dipping sauce.

Roasted Antipasto with Crostini

PHOTO ON PAGE 53

I love serving a good antipasto plate and always enjoy when a friend has taken the time to assemble one for a get-together. An assortment of fresh and marinated veggies, olives, cheese, salami, and whatever else you want is a perfect way to start enjoying the company of friends and family. I added a few roasted veggies to amp up the flavor.

1 medium eggplant, cut into 1-inch cubes (about 2 cups)

1 small fennel bulb, cut into ½- to 1-inch pieces

1 small red onion, cut into ½- to 1-inch pieces

5 tablespoons extra virgin olive oil, plus more for drizzling

2 tablespoons red wine vinegar

Kosher salt and freshly ground black pepper

1 cup cherry tomatoes, halved

½ cup pitted Castelvetrano olives, halved

One 12-ounce jar marinated artichoke hearts, drained

1 cup pickled mushrooms (page 57 or jarred marinated mushrooms), halved

1 baguette, cut into ⅓-inch slices

1 garlic clove

½ cup ciliegine mozzarella balls, halved

3 ounces Calabrese salami log, quartered and sliced

1 teaspoon chopped oregano

¼ cup chopped basil, plus whole leaves for garnish

Preheat the oven to 400°F. Line a baking sheet with parchment paper.

Combine the eggplant, fennel, and onion in a large bowl. Drizzle with 3 tablespoons of the olive oil and 1 tablespoon of the vinegar. Season with ½ teaspoon salt and ¼ teaspoon pepper and toss to combine. Spread the mixture evenly on the prepared baking sheet. Transfer to the oven and roast for 15 minutes, until the vegetables are just beginning to soften.

Remove the baking sheet from the oven and add the tomatoes, olives, artichoke hearts, mushrooms, and 1 tablespoon of the olive oil. Stir to combine. Return the baking sheet to the oven and roast for an additional 15 to 20 minutes, until the tomatoes are soft but still intact.

Meanwhile, prep the crostini. Arrange the sliced baguette on a baking sheet and drizzle with olive oil. Season with a pinch of salt. Transfer to the oven and toast for 10 minutes, until the bread is crisp and golden. Let cool slightly. When the crostini is cool enough to handle, rub the garlic on each slice. Set aside until the antipasto is ready.

Remove the vegetables from the oven and let cool for 10 minutes. After the vegetables have cooled slightly, transfer them to a bowl. Add the mozzarella, salami, oregano, basil, the remaining 1 tablespoon olive oil, and the remaining 1 tablespoon vinegar. Stir to combine. Season to taste with salt and pepper.

Transfer the antipasto to a serving bowl and garnish with whole basil leaves. Serve with crostini.

Zesty Cheddar Cheese Crackers

PHOTO ON PAGE 53

This is my version of Cheez-It crackers. They're a little bit of a challenge to make because you have to roll out the dough and shape it, but the effort is worth it: you'll have marvelous homemade crackers that will keep for several weeks in an airtight container.

1¼ cups all-purpose flour, plus more for dusting

1 cup freshly grated extra-sharp yellow Cheddar (about 4 ounces)

¾ teaspoon smoked paprika, plus more for dusting

Cayenne pepper

Kosher salt

½ stick (4 tablespoons) cold unsalted butter, cut into ½-inch cubes

½ cup heavy cream

Preheat the oven to 400°F. Line a baking sheet with parchment paper.

Combine the flour, Cheddar, smoked paprika, a pinch of cayenne, and ¾ teaspoon salt in a food processor and pulse to combine. Add the butter and pulse until incorporated. Add the cream and process until the dough forms into a ball.

Lightly dust a sheet of parchment paper with flour and place the dough on top. Shape the dough into a flat rectangle, then lightly dust it with flour. Use a rolling pin to roll it out until it is a little less than ¼ inch thick (about a 9 × 12-inch rectangle). Cut the dough into roughly 1- to 1½-inch squares or rectangles and carefully transfer to the prepared baking sheet. Sprinkle the dough pieces with about ¼ teaspoon more salt, gently pressing it into the surface, then dust very lightly with more smoked paprika.

Bake until light golden brown, 10 to 12 minutes. Let cool slightly, then transfer to a wire rack to cool completely.

Sausage and Olive Cheese Bites

My mom made sausage and cheese bites like these, and I think every woman of her generation knew how to whip up something similar, often with classic Bisquick and Jimmy Dean sausages. I still use Bisquick, but I prefer hot Italian sausage, provolone piccante (an aged, sharper version of provolone), and pitted Castelvetrano olives for extra flavor. I guarantee these will disappear before you can tell anyone how easy they were to make.

3 cups Bisquick Original Pancake & Baking Mix

1 pound bulk hot Italian sausage

2 cups freshly grated provolone piccante (about 8 ounces)

2 cups freshly grated Monterey Jack (about 8 ounces)

½ cup milk

1 teaspoon Italian seasoning

One 8 to 10-ounce jar pitted Castelvetrano olives, drained

Preheat the oven to 350°F. Line two baking sheets with parchment paper.

Add the Bisquick, Italian sausage, cheeses, milk, and Italian seasoning to a large bowl. Using clean hands or a silicone spatula, gently mix until no streaks of baking mix remain.

To make the bites, scoop a heaping tablespoon of the meat mixture into your hand. Gently flatten the mixture and place an olive in the center. Wrap the meat mixture around the olive and seal it by rolling it into a ball in your hands. Place the bite on the prepared baking sheet. Repeat with the remaining meat mixture and olives, placing the bites about ½ inch apart on the baking sheets.

Bake for 20 to 25 minutes, until golden brown. Transfer to a serving platter. Serve warm or at room temperature.

Smoky Salmon Dip

It was Ed who got me hooked on great fish dips. He loved any type of fish and crab dip, salted and pickled herring, and smoked oysters and mussels. This dip is easy: open a can of salmon, mix with cream cheese, and you're ready to party. The rice paper wrapper is a fancy touch.

8 ounces cream cheese, room temperature

One 5- to 6-ounce can salmon, drained and picked through for bones

2 green onions, chopped

¼ teaspoon liquid smoke

Kosher salt and freshly ground black pepper

Vegetable oil, for frying

5 rice paper wrappers

Add the cream cheese, salmon, green onions, and liquid smoke to a medium bowl. Use a silicone spatula to mix together until evenly combined. Season to taste with salt and pepper. Refrigerate until ready to serve.

Line a baking sheet with paper towels. Add enough oil to completely cover the base of a large skillet and heat over medium-high heat. Once the oil is shimmering, add a rice paper wrapper to the skillet. It should instantly puff up. Once puffed, flip and fry for a few more seconds. Transfer to the prepared baking sheet to drain. Repeat with the remaining wrappers.

Break the rice paper crackers into smaller pieces and arrange on a serving platter. Serve with the dip.

Steakhouse Shrimp Cocktail with Sauce Trio

Who doesn't love ordering shrimp cocktail in a steakhouse? It's a classic for a reason. I've provided recipes for three sauces, including a traditional spicy cocktail sauce, which is the way I like it. If you ask me, this is what it means to indulge.

For the Shrimp
1 lemon, halved

¼ cup parsley sprigs

2 garlic cloves, smashed

1 teaspoon kosher salt

10 black peppercorns

1 pound large shrimp, peeled and deveined

For the Spicy Cocktail Sauce
¾ cup ketchup

1 tablespoon chipotle in adobo sauce

1 teaspoon prepared horseradish

1 tablespoon freshly squeezed lemon juice

For the Lemon Basil Cocktail Sauce
½ cup sour cream

½ cup mayonnaise

2 tablespoons lemon zest

2 tablespoons chopped basil

¼ teaspoon kosher salt

¼ teaspoon freshly ground black pepper

For the Garlic Chili Sauce
¼ cup low-sodium soy sauce

1 teaspoon sesame oil

1 tablespoon rice vinegar

3 teaspoons Easy Garlic Chili Crisp (page 330 or store-bought chili crisp)

1 tablespoon grated ginger

1 garlic clove, grated

2 green onions, sliced

To poach the shrimp, fill a medium saucepan with 6 cups of water. Squeeze the juice from the halved lemon into the saucepan and then add the lemon halves. Add the parsley sprigs, garlic, salt, and peppercorns and bring to a simmer. Once the water is simmering, add the shrimp and cook until just opaque, 3 to 5 minutes. Remove the shrimp from the poaching liquid and chill completely.

To make the spicy cocktail sauce, whisk together the ketchup, adobo sauce, horseradish, and lemon juice in a small bowl.

To make the lemon basil cocktail sauce, whisk together the sour cream, mayo, lemon zest, basil, salt, and pepper in a small bowl.

To make the garlic chili sauce, whisk together the soy sauce, sesame oil, rice vinegar, chili crisp, ginger, garlic, and green onions in a small bowl.

To serve, cover a platter with crushed ice and arrange the shrimp on top. Serve with the sauces.

Thyme and Gruyère Savory Cookies

I'm going to warn you now: these fly off the plate. After you make them once, you'll probably want to double the recipe the next time. They are similar to shortbread but savory instead of sweet, and you can serve them as you would chips. They don't need a dip or a spread. But no one will complain if you do offer a little sumpin' sumpin'.

1 large egg

1 cup freshly grated Gruyère (about 4 ounces)

1 cup all-purpose flour, plus more for dusting

2 tablespoons fresh thyme leaves

1 teaspoon freshly ground black pepper

¼ teaspoon kosher salt

5 tablespoons cold unsalted butter, cut into ½-inch cubes

2 to 4 tablespoons ice water

Preheat the oven to 375°F. Line a baking sheet with parchment paper.

Whisk the egg with 1 tablespoon of water in a small bowl to make an egg wash. Set aside.

Combine the cheese, flour, thyme, pepper, and salt in a food processor. Pulse until the cheese is broken up and incorporated with the flour. Add the butter and pulse until you have pieces smaller than a pea, 10 to 15 pulses. While pulsing, stream in the ice water, 1 tablespoon at a time. After 2 tablespoons, remove the lid and check your dough; it should look like wet sand and hold together when you squeeze it. If it doesn't, place the lid back on and pulse in the remaining 1 to 2 tablespoons ice water.

Turn the dough out onto a lightly floured work surface and knead it a few times, just until it comes together. Lightly flour a rolling pin and roll the dough out until it's ¼ inch thick. Using a 2½-inch round cutter, cut out the cookies and place them 1 inch apart on the prepared baking sheet. Gather the dough scraps and lightly knead together. Continue the process of rolling out the dough and cutting cookies until all of the dough is used. Brush the cookies with the egg wash.

Bake for 12 to 14 minutes, until the cookies are lightly golden and puffed. Let cool for a few minutes before transferring to a wire rack to cool completely. Repeat with the remaining dough, always using a cool baking sheet.

SALADS

"With apologies to James Brown, *please*, *please*, *please* don't put the dressing on the side."

Burrata with Grilled Peaches

I debated whether this should be called a salad before deciding it didn't matter. It's simply delicious, period. Grilling peaches brings out a fresh, sweet flavor in this wonderfully juicy fruit. Paired with the creamy, soft texture of a good burrata and the lively nip of Calabrian chili paste, it's one of summer's yummiest romances.

3 firm-ripe peaches

4 tablespoons extra virgin olive oil

Kosher salt and freshly ground black pepper

1 tablespoon red wine vinegar

½ teaspoon Calabrian chili paste or red pepper flakes

8 ounces burrata

2 tablespoons small mint leaves

2 tablespoons torn basil leaves

Preheat a grill pan or outdoor grill to medium-high heat.

Quarter the peaches. Place the peaches in a large bowl and toss with 2 tablespoons of the olive oil and salt and pepper to taste. Grill the peach pieces, turning once, until charred on both sides, about 2 minutes per side.

Meanwhile, whisk together the vinegar, chili paste, and the remaining 2 tablespoons oil in the same bowl. Toss the grilled peaches in the dressing, then place on a serving platter. Nestle the burrata around the peaches and score the top with an X to expose the creamy insides.

Drizzle with the remaining dressing. Sprinkle with mint and basil.

Beverly Hills Chopped Salad

Though inspired by the fabled chopped salad at La Scala restaurant in Beverly Hills, this recipe is very close to the chopped salad my mom used to make—though she used her red wine vinaigrette. It's also similar to a sub sandwich, minus the bread. If the ingredients are chopped correctly, you can do as I often do and—don't laugh—eat it with a spoon.

1 head iceberg
    lettuce, chopped

1 romaine heart, chopped

5 ounces dry salami,
    julienned

One 15-ounce can chickpeas,
    drained and rinsed

2 vine-ripened tomatoes,
    seeds removed
    and chopped

1 cup freshly grated
    mozzarella (about 4 ounces)

⅓ cup extra virgin olive oil

⅓ cup white wine vinegar

1 teaspoon dry mustard

½ teaspoon kosher salt

½ teaspoon freshly ground
    black pepper

⅓ cup freshly grated
    Parmesan (about
    1½ ounces)

Place the iceberg, romaine, salami, chickpeas, tomatoes, and mozzarella in a large salad bowl.

Whisk together the olive oil, vinegar, dry mustard, salt, pepper, and Parmesan in a measuring cup or mason jar.

Pour the dressing over the salad and toss to combine. Serve immediately.

California Cobb

I love a one-dish meal, and this recipe is exactly that. This delicious salad can be made in one bowl, or for an especially stunning presentation, I recommend arranging all the ingredients on a platter. It's the picture of freshness, good health, and nature's bounty, and you won't be able to wait to dig in.

4 cups roughly chopped romaine heart (1 heart)

¾ cup cooked red quinoa

Blue Cheese Dressing (page 321)

5 slices cooked bacon, cut into 1-inch pieces

2 hard-boiled eggs, quartered

1 cup small heirloom cherry tomatoes, halved (about 8 ounces)

1 small avocado, cut into 1-inch chunks

1 small watermelon radish, thinly sliced and then quartered

Toss the romaine and quinoa with 2 tablespoons of the dressing in a serving bowl. Arrange the bacon, eggs, tomatoes, avocados, and radish in even sections over the top. Drizzle with more dressing and serve immediately.

Chicken Salad

A good, fresh chicken salad seasoned to perfection is my definition of indulgence. And trust me, this is a very good recipe. Consider this your base, then let your imagination and taste buds go wild as far as adding ingredients you love. Use your convenient meal prep chicken or pick up a delicious rotisserie chicken from the grocery store and get all that juicy white and dark meat while it's still warm.

Heaping ⅓ cup mayonnaise

½ teaspoon garlic powder

½ teaspoon onion powder

2 tablespoons freshly squeezed lemon juice

1 tablespoon chopped dill

1 tablespoon chopped cilantro

Kosher salt and freshly ground black pepper

2 cups cooked diced chicken (white and dark meat; or use Meal Prep Chicken Breasts, page 191)

1 celery stalk, finely diced

1 small carrot, coarsely grated

⅓ cup diced Honeycrisp apple (from ½ apple)

1 green onion, thinly sliced

¼ cup roughly chopped pecans

Whisk together the mayo, garlic powder, onion powder, lemon juice, dill, cilantro, ½ teaspoon salt, and ¼ teaspoon pepper in a large bowl until evenly combined.

Add the chicken, celery, carrot, apple, green onion, and pecans to the bowl with the dressing and mix to combine. Season to taste with salt and pepper.

Chicken salad is so versatile, you can really use whatever you have on hand to create a delicious dish. Here are some other great additions to jazz up any chicken salad:

- curry powder
- diced bell pepper
- diced pickled jalapeños
- ranch seasoning
- chopped hard-boiled egg
- diced radishes
- roasted corn kernels
- dried fruit (cranberries, currants, raisins, dates)

- quartered grapes
- chopped arugula
- chopped blanched broccoli
- roasted cubed sweet potato
- substitute Greek yogurt for mayonnaise

Cook's Note

Cold Poached Salmon Nicoise Salad

When you poach salmon in wine, herbs, and other seasonings, it's good to eat on its own. But when you put it on a bed of lettuce with potatoes, haricots verts, hard-boiled eggs, tomatoes, and olives, it becomes a sensational lunch or dinner. Light but filling and oh so delicious. Feel free to substitute leftover grilled or roasted salmon.

For the Salmon

- 1 cup dry white wine
- 1 tablespoon Dijon mustard
- 5 dill sprigs
- 2 lemons, 1 halved, the other sliced into thin rounds
- 1 pound skin-on salmon, pin bones removed
- Kosher salt and freshly ground black pepper

For the Dressing

- ⅓ cup white wine vinegar
- ¼ cup extra virgin olive oil
- 1 teaspoon chopped dill
- 1 teaspoon Dijon mustard
- ¼ teaspoon garlic powder
- ½ teaspoon kosher salt
- ½ teaspoon freshly ground black pepper

For the Salad

- 1 pound baby Yukon Gold potatoes
- Kosher salt and freshly ground black pepper
- 4 large eggs
- 8 ounces haricots verts or thin green beans, trimmed

To make the salmon, combine the wine, mustard, dill, and 1 cup of water in a large straight-sided skillet. Squeeze the juice from the halved lemon into the skillet and then add the lemon halves. Bring the mixture to a simmer over medium heat. Sprinkle the salmon with a generous pinch of salt and pepper. Once the liquid is simmering, gently add the salmon, skin side down, and reduce the heat to low. Place the lemon slices on top of the salmon, cover the pan, and cook for 10 minutes. Remove from the heat and let sit, covered, for 5 minutes. The salmon should flake easily with a fork. Carefully transfer the salmon to a plate. Let cool completely.

To make the dressing, combine the vinegar, olive oil, dill, mustard, garlic powder, salt, and pepper in a jar with a lid. Cover and shake to emulsify. Set aside until ready to assemble the salad.

To make the salad, place the potatoes in a large saucepan with enough cold water to cover by 4 inches. Add a big pinch of salt and bring to a boil over medium-high heat. Cook until the potatoes are fork-tender, 5 to 8 minutes. Use a slotted spoon to transfer the potatoes to a plate. Reserve the pot with boiling water to use to cook the eggs and haricots verts.

Fill a large bowl with ice and water. Bring the water back up to a boil, if needed, then add the eggs and cook for 7 minutes. Transfer the eggs to the ice bath. Return the water to a boil and add the haricots verts. Cook until they are crisp-tender, about 3 minutes. Transfer to the ice bath. Remove the eggs from the ice bath, peel, and set aside. Drain the beans, cut them into thirds, and set aside until ready to assemble.

Using the flat base of a measuring cup or a glass, lightly smash the potatoes to expose some of the flesh. Sprinkle with

¼ cup extra virgin olive oil

1 large head frisée lettuce,
   cut into bite-size pieces
   (about 5 cups)

1 romaine heart, cut into bite-
   size pieces (about 3 cups)

1 cup cherry tomatoes, halved

½ cup pitted
   kalamata olives, halved

a generous pinch of salt and pepper. Heat a large skillet over medium-high heat. Add the olive oil and swirl to coat the pan. Carefully add the potatoes seasoning side down. Sprinkle the unseasoned side of the potatoes with salt and pepper and cook until they are crispy and golden brown in places, about 4 minutes per side. Some potatoes may break apart—that's totally fine! Transfer to a plate and set aside until ready to assemble.

To assemble the salad, arrange the frisée and romaine on a large platter. Drizzle with about half of the dressing and toss to coat. Top with the crispy potatoes, haricots verts, tomatoes, and olives. Flake the cooled salmon into large pieces and scatter it on top of the salad. Slice the eggs in half and nestle into the salad. Drizzle with the remaining dressing and serve.

Cress Salad

I love watercress and its more delicate doppelgänger, upland cress. To me, both are like arugula, only the watercress is amped up to be super peppery and the upland cress used in this recipe is slightly less pungent. This salad is wonderful and light, with a bold, salty flavor that pairs well with just about anything.

¼ cup extra virgin olive oil

3 tablespoons freshly squeezed lemon juice

1 teaspoon Dijon mustard

½ teaspoon kosher salt

2 bunches upland cress, roots removed

1 green pear, cut into chunky matchsticks

½ cup roughly chopped basil

⅓ cup pitted kalamata olives, sliced

⅓ cup shaved Manchego

Flaky sea salt, for garnish

Combine the olive oil, lemon juice, mustard, and kosher salt in a jar with a lid. Cover and shake to emulsify.

Toss the cress, pear, basil, and olives with the dressing in a large salad bowl. Top with the Manchego and toss lightly again. Garnish with flaky salt and serve immediately.

Crispy Goat Cheese Salad

You'd have to be a much better writer than I to re-create the indelible excitement of a first kiss, but I can share the first time I tasted crispy goat cheese in a restaurant, back in the 1980s. It was still slightly warm and melted in my mouth with a deliciousness that I remember to this very day. I hope this retro classic resonates the same way with you.

8 ounces goat cheese (in a log)

3 tablespoons all-purpose flour

1 large egg

¼ cup panko bread crumbs

¼ teaspoon Italian seasoning

¼ teaspoon paprika

¼ teaspoon garlic powder

¼ teaspoon onion powder

¼ teaspoon freshly ground black pepper

2 tablespoons extra virgin olive oil

1 Honeycrisp apple

1 tablespoon freshly squeezed lemon juice

5 ounces baby spring mix

Red Wine Vinaigrette (page 325)

½ cup toasted walnuts, roughly chopped

Line a plate with parchment paper. Cut the goat cheese into four equal rounds. If the cheese crumbles, just gently form it back into a round using your hands. Place the rounds on the parchment-lined plate and transfer to the fridge while you prep the rest of your ingredients.

Set up your dredging station. Add the flour to a shallow bowl. Add the egg and a small splash of water to another shallow bowl and whisk to combine. In a third shallow bowl, whisk together the panko, Italian seasoning, paprika, garlic powder, onion powder, and pepper.

Remove the goat cheese from the fridge. Starting with one round, dredge it in the flour, making sure it's fully coated before shaking off any excess. Next, transfer to the egg mixture, again making sure it's fully coated before letting any excess drip off. Finally, transfer to the panko mixture, gently pressing so the crumbs stick and completely cover the cheese. Set the coated goat cheese back on the parchment-lined plate and repeat with the remaining three rounds.

Line a plate with paper towels. Heat the olive oil in a small nonstick skillet over medium heat. Once the oil is hot, add the goat cheese rounds to the pan in an even layer. Cook until lightly golden, 30 seconds to 1 minute. Flip and continue cooking until golden on the other side, an additional 30 seconds to 1 minute. Transfer to the paper towel–lined plate to drain.

Core and thinly slice the apple. Place the apple slices in a small bowl and drizzle with the lemon juice. This helps prevent browning and also adds lots of flavor.

To assemble the salad, toss the spring mix and vinaigrette in a large bowl. Evenly divide the salad among four plates. Arrange the apple slices on each salad, sprinkle with the walnuts, and top with a crispy goat cheese round. Serve immediately.

Elote Salad

Loosely translated, the Spanish word *elote* means "fresh ear of corn." This recipe turns that ear into a salad that just bursts with freshness and flavor, like the amazing street corn I've had on my travels. This is an easy version to make, and you don't have to worry about walking around with corn on the cob and getting it all over your face. Pair it with grilled chicken or a delicious fillet of salmon (or salmon burger)!

1 tablespoon vegetable oil

1 tablespoon unsalted butter

3 cups fresh sweet corn
(from 4 large ears)

1 shallot, diced

3 garlic cloves, grated

Kosher salt

½ cup sliced green onions
(from 1 bunch)

1 Fresno chile, finely chopped

¼ cup chopped cilantro

Zest and juice of 1 lime

2 tablespoons mayonnaise

¼ cup crumbled cotija

Chili powder, for garnish

Heat a large nonstick skillet over medium-high heat. Add the oil and butter. Once the butter has melted, add the corn and stir to coat it in the butter mixture. Spread the corn into an even layer and cook, undisturbed, until the corn is slightly browned, 3 to 4 minutes. Add the shallot and stir to combine. Cook until the shallot has softened, another 3 minutes. Add the garlic and ½ teaspoon salt. Stir to combine, and cook until the garlic is fragrant, about 30 seconds. Remove from the heat.

Transfer the corn to a large serving bowl. Add the green onions, Fresno chile, cilantro, lime zest and juice, mayo, and 2 tablespoons of the cotija. Stir to combine and season with salt to taste. Top with the remaining 2 tablespoons cotija, garnish with chili powder, and serve immediately.

Frisée Salad

My friend, the great chef Ludo Lefebvre, offers a frisée salad at his French bistro Petite Trois, and it's a dish I go there to indulge in all by itself. It's that special. But because I can't always go there, I made my own version as a treat to myself. I find the entire process relaxing and the finished salad a deserved reward.

6 ounces slab bacon, cut into ¼-inch strips (or use thick-sliced bacon cut into ¼-inch strips)

2 tablespoons distilled white vinegar

4 large eggs

6 cups frisée lettuce

For the Dressing

¼ cup extra virgin olive oil

¼ cup champagne vinegar

2 tablespoons minced shallot

2 teaspoons Dijon mustard

Kosher salt and freshly ground black pepper

Place the bacon lardons in a cold medium skillet and turn the heat to medium. Cook, stirring frequently, until the lardons are crispy and the fat has rendered, 5 to 7 minutes. Use a slotted spoon to transfer the lardons to a paper towel–lined plate and set aside.

To poach the eggs, fill a wide, shallow pot with about 3 inches of water. Bring to a brisk simmer and add the white vinegar. Crack the eggs into separate small bowls or ramekins, then gently slide the eggs into the simmering water. Cook at a gentle simmer until the whites are set but the yolks are still runny, 2 to 3 minutes. Gently remove the eggs using a slotted spoon and place on a paper towel–lined plate to drain.

To make the dressing, combine the olive oil, champagne vinegar, shallot, and mustard in a jar with a lid. Cover and shake to emulsify. Season to taste with salt and pepper.

To assemble, toss the frisée and dressing in a large salad bowl. Evenly divide the salad among four plates. Top the salads with the lardons and poached eggs. Garnish with extra pepper.

Grapefruit Salad

This refreshing salad is inspired by my friend Beth, who makes it with my Green Goddess Dressing (page 324) for herself and her husband and for guests when they entertain. She also adds sliced hearts of palm, which is delicious. I have paired the salad here with my Honey Mustard Dressing as a way of bringing the grapefruit and avocado together with a little more zip. While supreming the fruit (removing the rind and pith) may take a little extra time, it is so worth it.

½ red onion, thinly sliced

2 red grapefruits

1 head butter lettuce, torn
    into bite-size pieces

1 avocado, diced

¼ cup smoked almonds,
    roughly chopped

Honey Mustard Dressing
    (page 327)

Place the onion in a small bowl and cover with cold water. Let sit for 5 minutes, then drain and dry.

To supreme a grapefruit, use a sharp knife to trim the top and bottom. Place it cut side down on a cutting board. Slice lengthwise between the flesh and the peel, following the fruit's contour and removing the peel and the pith. Pick up the grapefruit and delicately slice between a segment and the membrane until you reach the center of the fruit. Make another slice on the other side of the segment to release it. Continue all the way around the grapefruit. Add the segments to a bowl and repeat with the second grapefruit.

To assemble the salad, place the lettuce in a large serving bowl. Top with the onion, avocado, grapefruit supremes, and almonds. Drizzle with the dressing and toss gently to combine. Serve immediately.

Kale and Sweet Potato Salad

This recipe came to me one day when I was hungry and my body was begging for fuel, not junk food. I needed a meal that would nourish me and rev me up—a forkful of feel-good and energy. I opened the fridge and put together all these great ingredients, and the Dill Pickle Vinaigrette sent it over the top. Indulge!

1 bunch lacinato kale, ribs removed, thinly sliced

1 tablespoon extra virgin olive oil

1 tablespoon freshly squeezed lemon juice

Kosher salt and freshly ground black pepper

2 cups finely shredded cabbage

1½ cups roasted diced sweet potato (from 1 sweet potato)

1 Honeycrisp or Pink Lady apple, diced

1 cup cooked tricolor quinoa

Dill Pickle Vinaigrette (page 327)

Toss the kale in a large salad bowl with the olive oil, lemon juice, and a pinch of salt and pepper. Use clean hands to massage the kale for 30 seconds to 1 minute. The kale will soften and turn a deep shiny green.

Add the cabbage, sweet potato, apple, and quinoa to the bowl and toss to combine. Add your desired amount of vinaigrette and toss to coat. Season to taste with salt and pepper. Serve immediately or refrigerate. The salad will last in the fridge for up to 2 days.

Mom's Waldorf Salad

I guess Freud was right; everything goes back to our childhood. My mom made a Waldorf salad when I was a little kid, and I loved that it was crunchy and sweet. It's still a refreshing change-of-pace way to serve a salad, and its association—going back to the 1890s—with New York's fabled Waldorf Astoria Hotel adds a touch of fancy pants to your table.

¾ cup buttermilk

¼ cup plus 2 teaspoons
   mayonnaise

3 tablespoons
   chopped chives

1 tablespoon plus 2 teaspoons
   apple cider vinegar

1 tablespoon sugar

1 lemon, juiced

Kosher salt and freshly
   ground black pepper

1 cup toasted walnuts,
   roughly chopped

8 celery stalks, sliced about
   ¼ inch thick on the bias

2 Gala apples, skin on, cored
   and diced

Whisk together the buttermilk, mayo, chives, vinegar, sugar, lemon juice, and ½ teaspoon each salt and pepper in a small bowl. Combine the walnuts, celery, and apples in a separate large bowl. Pour three-quarters of the dressing over the celery-apple mixture and toss to coat. Let stand for 5 minutes at room temperature, then toss again. Adjust the seasoning as desired. Add the remaining dressing and toss again. Serve at room temperature.

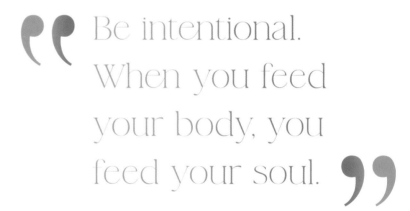

"Be intentional. When you feed your body, you feed your soul."

Roasted Tomato Panzanella

When the tomatoes in my garden go crazy in the summer, I love making panzanella. Roasting the tomatoes brings out their amazing flavor. To me, this dish confirms that the best ingredients are the freshest, and that often means taking advantage of what is in season. This salad pairs well with chicken or fish but is also great all by itself. I recommend an outdoor table and a setting sun.

½ loaf day-old ciabatta bread, torn into 1- to 1½-inch cubes (about 6 cups)

3 cups multicolor cherry tomatoes

2 orange bell peppers, cut into ½-inch strips

½ red onion, cut into ⅓-inch slices

2 tablespoons extra virgin olive oil

Kosher salt and freshly ground black pepper

⅓ cup pitted kalamata olives, halved

Red Wine Vinaigrette (page 325)

¼ cup chopped basil, plus whole basil leaves for garnish

Flaky sea salt, for garnish

Preheat the oven to 400°F. Line two baking sheets with parchment paper.

Place the torn bread on one of the prepared baking sheets. Place the tomatoes, bell pepper, and onion on the other. Drizzle the vegetables with the olive oil and season generously with kosher salt and black pepper. Toss to coat the vegetables in the seasoning. Transfer both baking sheets to the oven and bake for 15 minutes. After 15 minutes, remove the bread; it should be crisp and lightly browned. Let cool while the vegetables continue to cook for an additional 10 to 15 minutes, until the tomatoes are bursting and the peppers and onions are soft.

Toss the bread and olives with the vinaigrette in a large salad bowl. Add the roasted vegetables and chopped basil and toss gently, being careful not to crush all the tomatoes. Garnish with basil leaves, flaky salt, and black pepper.

Romaine Heart Caesar

I know you don't need help making a Caesar salad, but this is me being indulgent by serving each person their own romaine heart. It's different, and it's a little fancy. Who doesn't like that?

2 tablespoons extra virgin olive oil

2 slices French bread, torn into small (⅓-inch) pieces (about 1 cup)

¼ teaspoon garlic powder

Kosher salt and freshly ground black pepper

2 romaine hearts

Lemon Caesar Dressing (page 324)

⅓ cup shaved Parmesan

Lemon wedges, for garnish

Heat the olive oil in a small saucepan over medium heat. Once the oil is hot, add the torn bread, garlic powder, ¼ teaspoon salt, and ¼ teaspoon pepper and toss to coat. Cook, tossing frequently, until the bread is crisp and golden, 3 to 5 minutes. Transfer the croutons to a plate to cool slightly.

Trim a bit of the root from the romaine and remove any limp or discolored outer leaves. Cut the romaine lengthwise and arrange on a platter. Top with the dressing, croutons, shaved Parmesan, and pepper. Garnish with lemon wedges. Serve immediately.

Three-Bean Salad on Toast

Do you ever do something for no other reason than that you love it? Do you need another reason? I love a good piece of toast. I also love a delicious three-bean salad. I combined the two the way I used to smush my Barbie and Ken dolls together. It's all about love, remember?

Extra virgin olive oil

3 tablespoons red
    wine vinegar

1 teaspoon Dijon mustard

½ teaspoon lemon zest

1 tablespoon freshly squeezed
    lemon juice

1 small garlic clove, grated

½ teaspoon Italian seasoning

Kosher salt and freshly
    ground black pepper

One 15-ounce can cannellini
    beans, drained and rinsed

One 15-ounce can chickpeas,
    drained and rinsed

One 15-ounce can black-eyed
    peas, drained and rinsed

2 celery stalks,
    finely chopped

2 tablespoons chopped
    celery leaves, plus more
    for garnish

1 shallot, finely chopped

2 tablespoons
    chopped parsley

2 tablespoons
    chopped chives

2 tablespoons chopped basil

4 slices Italian bread

Flaky sea salt, for garnish

Lemon wedges, for serving
    (optional)

Whisk together ¼ cup of olive oil, the vinegar, mustard, lemon zest and juice, garlic, Italian seasoning, ½ teaspoon kosher salt, and ¼ teaspoon pepper in a large bowl. Add the beans, celery, celery leaves, shallot, and herbs to the bowl and toss to combine with the dressing. Set aside.

Heat a large nonstick skillet over medium heat with enough olive oil to lightly coat the bottom. Once the oil shimmers gently, add the bread in an even layer and cook until golden brown and crisp, about 2 minutes. Flip and cook until crispy on the other side, an additional 1 to 2 minutes. Transfer to a paper towel–lined plate to drain. Season with a pinch of kosher salt.

To serve, spoon the bean salad on top of the toast and garnish with celery leaves, flaky salt, and pepper. Serve with a lemon wedge, if desired.

Store any leftover bean salad in an airtight container in the fridge for up to 5 days.

Don't Be Afraid to Ask Questions

Way back in the 1980s, which is now so long ago I can't do the math to figure out exactly how long ago it was, a *People* magazine profile of me mentioned that I had a leather-bound collection of the 100 Greatest Books Ever Written, but I was self-conscious that I hadn't read any of them. That has changed. I've read a few since then and turned into someone who always has a book going. But as I have grown older, I've grown bolder and less insecure about what I don't know or can do better. One time I watched my friend, the great chef Ludo Lefebvre, make an omelet (no one makes an omelet like the French), and all I could say was "How did you do that?" Before I got to Food Network, I put olive oil in my pasta water. Then Giada De Laurentiis and Alex Guarnaschelli said no, all that does is make your pasta slippery. Use salt instead—and be generous. It flavors the pasta.

There is always more to learn, and the only way to do so is to keep an open mind, stay curious, and ask questions—without any fear of being embarrassed. I remember discovering a new cheese store in my neighborhood. I walked into The Cheesemonger, immediately stopped to inhale the rich, vibrant aroma filling the shop, and asked the couple behind the counter how long they'd been in business. "Eight years," they said. I laughed at myself for thinking they had recently opened. Typical. How many thousands of times must I have driven past this adorable shop without noticing it? But I think you see things when you need to, like a new nail polish color or a clever hack to cube avocados or clean the stovetop. Suddenly, it's voilà, exactly what I wanted! Today it was all about cheese.

I was greeted by a display case filled with small wedges and rounds of cheeses with names like Hornbacher, Chällerhocker, Chabichou d'Antan, Chiriboga Blue, Colston Bassett Stilton, Garrotxa, and Ossau-Iraty Fermier. I thought I knew enough about cheese, but this was a new language to me, and fun, and I had questions! Lots of questions. I know this is true of most people when it comes to artisanal cheeses. We love the idea of them, and they taste even better, but we don't speak the language. Fortunately for me, owners Kia and Tyler Burton, a former college professor and classical musician, respectively, were used to sharing their passion and expertise with people walking into their shop with a range of knowledge, from connoisseurs of small-batch cheeses to those like me who were enthusiastic but confused. "Either way, we try to guide them," said Kia. "We say, 'Tell us what you like,' and then we narrow it down

to soft or firm, sweet or sharp, nutty or funky." Tyler placed a shaving of Cheddar that had been aged seven years in front of me and said, "Then we taste." It was delicious, buttery, with a little kick. "Everyone likes Cheddar," he said. "It's a good place to start. Then you work your way out."

I tried a smidge of soft Époisses (before serving, you want to let it get to room temperature, then just dip bread into it, and free yourself to revel in the thick, nutty, and yes, stinky deliciousness); a slice of Gouda made from cow, sheep, goat, and water buffalo milk, which was new to me but after tasting it, I instantly imagined using to make a super grilled cheese sandwich; and finally we tried a Cana de Cabra from Spain, a bloomy-rind goat's milk cheese that was like an unusual Brie—semisoft, with a white mold on the outside and two layers inside, a soft area that's the ripest and a slightly firmer center that has a cakey texture. I tasted hints of lemon, herbs, and black pepper. I was reminded that cheese is as complicated and nuanced as wine. There are all different kinds of milks (cow, sheep, goat, and water buffalo), textures, and tastes, along with terms like "washed" and "bloomy," and varieties like Cheddar, Gouda, Alpine, and Swiss. You have cheese makers from around the world. Ask questions. I learned that soft, delicate cheeses should be eaten within a few days and harder cheeses naturally keep longer. Before leaving, I asked which cheeses they recommended for a starter versus a cheese plate for dessert.

"Great question," Kia said. "You can find people who will give you rules, but I've never differentiated between the two. It's more about what you pair them with. A first course or appetizer will have some charcuterie and olives. At the end of the meal, you will have some grapes or apples and pears, depending on what's in season, and maybe some sweet wine. You can't go wrong." Sadly, a few months after this visit, this lovely shop shuttered its doors, bidding the neighborhood a sweet goodbye. I wish I had discovered them sooner, but I cherish the expertise and passion they shared with me. And at the risk of being redundant, that exemplifies the point I keep returning to here. It's the connection food allows us to make with each other. Thank you, Kia and Tyler, and best of luck on your next delicious endeavor. Now on to the wine store!

CHEESE & CHARCUTERIE

"Now they're called 'girl dinners.' But I have loved cheese and charcuterie plates since I was a little kid cutting up bologna, provolone, pepperoni, olives, and pickles and arranging them on my own plate.

"To this day, nothing says, 'Hello, this is going to be a good time,' like a cheese and charcuterie board.

"It's a great way to express yourself artistically."

Cheese Board How-To

RULES TO GO BY

- You'll need about 3 ounces of cheese per person for an appetizer board, but double that if you plan on serving it as a meal.
- Choose a mixture of textures: soft, semisoft, firm, hard.
- To create an eye-catching board, present the cheese in different ways. Soft cheese should be left whole and served with a cheese knife, semisoft cheese can be served with a cheese knife or slicer, firm cheese can be sliced into shapes like rectangles and triangles, and hard cheese can be broken into hunks.
- A cheese board can be an appetizer or a dessert! You can even repurpose your appetizer board for the dessert course by adding some extra fresh or dried fruit and some chocolate-covered nuts, or the Chocolate Peanut Butter Dates (page 289)!

Soft Cheese

Brie: mild, creamy, and buttery with an edible rind

Camembert: similar to Brie but slightly sharper, with a nutty flavor

Chèvre: goat cheese; a sharp, tangy flavor

Gorgonzola Dolce: blue cheese; a nutty, pungent taste

Semisoft Cheese

Manchego: sweet, salty, nutty flavor with a slightly crumbly texture

Fontina: mild and buttery

Gouda: rich and nutty; also comes in a smoked variety that is slightly firmer

Roquefort: sweet and pungent with a slightly metallic taste

Firm Cheese

Cheddar: aged Cheddars can be nutty and crumbly with a granular texture, while a mild Cheddar will have a smooth, creamy finish

Gruyère: rich, salty, creamy, and nutty

Emmental: buttery and slightly fruity

Hard Cheese

Parmigiano-Reggiano: rich, tangy, and nutty with a granular texture

Pecorino Romano: similar to Parmigiano-Reggiano but slightly softer and saltier

Mimolette: bright orange in color, with a sweet, buttery flavor

Grana Padano: similar to Parmigiano-Reggiano but with a milder, sweeter flavor

Piave: a slightly sweet cousin of Parmigiano-Reggiano

Extras

Fresh fruit, such as apples, pears, berries, melon

Dried fruit, such as apricots, plums, apples, cranberries

Spreads, such as fig jam, quince paste, tapenade, mango chutney, pepper jelly, mustards

Olives

Pickled vegetables

Cornichons

Sliced baguette

Crackers

Italian breadsticks (grissini)

Mixed nuts

Chocolate-covered almonds

Chocolate Peanut Butter Dates (page 289)

Charcuterie How-To

RULES TO GO BY

- You'll need about 3 ounces of meat per person for an appetizer charcuterie board, but double that if you're planning on serving it as a meal.
- Pick three to five different kinds of meat, depending on how many people you are serving.
- Present the meat in different ways: small logs of salami can be sliced into thick coins, larger salami can be purchased thinly sliced and folded to create volume, and prosciutto can be swirled so that it's easy to pick up.
- Don't limit yourself to sliced deli meats; you can also include pâtés and rillettes on your charcuterie board.

Dry-Cured Meats

Prosciutto: fatty with a sweet, salty, and delicate flavor

Bresaola: deep red in color with a lean, meaty flavor

Serrano ham: similar to prosciutto but slightly drier in texture and deeper in color

Ibérico ham: well marbled with an earthy, grassy, slightly nutty flavor

Capicola: salty, slightly spicy, and smoky

Salami

Genoa: classic, mild, with hints of garlic

Soppressata: spiced with red pepper flakes and black peppercorns

Pepperoni: smoky, spicy, and slightly sweet

Finocchiona: spiced with fennel

Peppered salami: encased in black pepper

Calabrese: comes two ways, dolce and piccante

Chorizo: Spanish style, spicy, and slightly sweet

Cooked Cured Meats / Spreads

Prosciutto cotto: very mild, slightly fatty

Mortadella: similar to bologna, sometimes dotted with pistachios or black peppercorns

Chicken liver pâté: rich and flavorful

Rillettes: duck, pork, and chicken have a concentrated, rich flavor

Extras

Nuts, such as Marcona almonds, smoked almonds, cashews, pecans, walnuts, mixed bar nuts

Crackers / crisps / breadsticks

Sliced baguette or crostini

Fresh vegetables, such as sliced cucumber, sliced carrot, endive, sliced fennel, radishes

Spreads, such as mustards, jams, mostarda, Tapenade (page 334)

Capers and caperberries

Pickled vegetables

Cornichons

Olives

Marinated artichokes

Roasted peppers

Planning a Menu

WHAT DO I FEEL LIKE?

As I sit down to plan a dinner menu, I often wonder what I really feel like eating that night. It's not always an easy question to answer, but that's part of the fun, isn't it? Sometimes I envy those who know exactly what they want, but most of the time I enjoy the process of figuring it out.

If I'm cooking for myself, I ask, *What does my body need? What is it telling me it wants? How do I want to feel after I eat?* And if I'm cooking for others, I ask, *What do I want to say to them?* Maybe I just want something fresh and crunchy. If I'm stressed, I might opt for something light and healthy, like fish and veggies. But if I'm in the mood for a treat, a juicy steak with sautéed mushrooms and greens is just the thing. And let's not forget about special occasions. When I went to my friend Suzanne's for Christmas dinner, I brought a decadent chocolate cake with cream cheese frosting. It was my way of showing her how much I appreciated her invitation.

The generations of women in my family who came before me planned their daily menus with practicality and a budget. They also knew everyone's favorites. I don't ever remember hearing complaints. Curious how the pros did it, I visited Bub & Grandma's, a popular new breakfast and lunch restaurant near my house started by former advertising writer Andy Kadin, one of LA's most revered bread bakers. I ordered an Italian sub, and Andy had a roast turkey sandwich. After my first mouthwatering bite, I said, "Mayo and mustard?" Andy nodded. "It's not the Italian I grew up with in New Jersey," he said. "But this is what we like. We're doing our own thing."

And doing it superbly. In 2015, Andy moved to LA with the idea of opening a sandwich shop, like a Subway or a Jersey Mike's. But when he was unable to find bread to his liking ("A great sandwich is all about the bread," he said, and I agree), he started making his own in his apartment kitchen. That effort turned into the bread bakery Bub & Grandma's—named after his two grandmothers—which became a hit with local restaurants and found the self-taught baker making up to thirty varieties of bread each day. Seven years later, he finally opened his own similarly named sandwich restaurant. That whole time Andy worked on Bub & Grandma's menu. "It was all about what me and my chef loved when we were kids," he said.

Hearing that, I knew I'd met a kindred spirit. "I knew an Italian sub had to be on the menu, and it had to be perfected," he explained. "The Turkey Trot was like a deli sandwich I had in high school. A tuna sandwich was important, and it had to include iceberg lettuce for the crunch. Without it, you have mush—and no one wants just mush."

As we continued to talk, he mentioned delis and sandwich shops he'd frequented as a kid in New Jersey, and then later when he was living and working in New York City. He spoke about keeping the menu focused—another good tip. He mentioned specials and surprises—a matzo ball soup on the weekend and a meatball sandwich being developed. He also talked about the joy of working with friends—both his head chef and pastry chef are longtime pals—and trusting his gut (and taste buds). "Nothing goes on the menu that we don't love ourselves," he said. So how do you plan a menu? Do your own thing. Use only fresh, quality ingredients. Find inspiration in favorites from your past. And make sure you love whatever you make.

BREAD

"The smell of fresh bread
baking fills a house with
delicious memories of
my nonnie and mom
and lots of love."

Bertinelli
Bread Dough

(page 122)

Nonnie's Crescia

This Italian classic is a treasured recipe of mine that's been passed down through the generations. I've always known it as my grandmother's flatbread, and I'm sure she learned to make it from her mother, and her mother learned it the same way. The key is to slather the dough generously with high-quality olive oil and sprinkle the finishing salt to taste. I always go for a depth of flavor that I hope would make my grandmother proud.

For the Bread Dough

¾ cup lukewarm water (about 105°F)

2 teaspoons honey

2 tablespoons extra virgin olive oil, plus more for greasing

2 cups all-purpose flour, plus more for dusting

One ¼-ounce packet instant yeast (2¼ teaspoons)

1 teaspoon kosher salt

For Assembly

2 tablespoons extra virgin olive oil

¼ medium yellow onion, thinly sliced

Kosher salt

To make the dough, combine the water, honey, and olive oil in a 2-cup measuring cup and stir to dissolve the honey. Set aside.

Whisk together the flour, yeast, and salt in the bowl of a stand mixer. Add the water mixture and mix with a silicone spatula until the dough becomes very shaggy. Attach the bowl to the stand mixer fitted with the dough hook and mix on medium speed until the dough has pulled away from the sides of the bowl and is elastic and slightly sticky to the touch, about 5 minutes.

Lightly drizzle a medium bowl with olive oil. Transfer the dough to the bowl and turn it to coat it in the oil. Cover with a clean kitchen towel and let rise in a warm place until doubled in size, about 1 hour.

Punch the dough down once to release some of the air bubbles. Lightly flour a clean work surface and your hands. Transfer the dough to the floured work surface and form it into a ball. Place the ball seam side down and lightly dust it with flour. Cover with a kitchen towel and let sit until slightly puffed, 15 to 30 minutes.

Meanwhile, preheat the oven to 450°F. Line a baking sheet with parchment paper.

Uncover the dough and lightly flour your hands and a rolling pin. Begin to stretch the dough with your hands, then switch to the rolling pin to help you stretch it into an oval that is about 11 × 14 inches. It's okay if the dough isn't completely even and has thinner spots; this helps to create a great crunchy texture. If the dough rips, just pinch it back together—it's meant to look rustic!

To assemble, transfer the stretched dough to the prepared

baking sheet. Use a pastry brush to coat the dough with the olive oil. Scatter the onion all over the dough and season generously with salt.

Bake for 15 to 17 minutes, until the bread is golden brown and the onion is beginning to char on the edges.

Transfer to a cutting board and cut as desired.

Multigrain Cinnamon Raisin Bread

When I was growing up, my mother occasionally spiced up her basic bread recipe with cinnamon and raisins. My mouth would start to water as soon as I caught the sweet smell of the loaf baking. I'm savoring those memories right now. Occasionally, as a treat, she made French toast with it.

½ cup old-fashioned rolled oats

1¾ cups boiling water

1¼ cups whole wheat flour

2 cups all-purpose flour, plus more for dusting

1 teaspoon kosher salt

1 tablespoon ground cinnamon

One ¼-ounce packet instant yeast (2¼ teaspoons)

3 tablespoons honey

3 tablespoons unsalted butter, melted and cooled to room temperature

¼ cup raisins

¼ cup golden raisins

1 tablespoon extra virgin olive oil

Cooking spray

1 large egg

Place the oats in the bowl of a stand mixer and cover with the boiling water. Let sit until the water reaches 105°F on an instant-read thermometer, 20 to 30 minutes.

Whisk together the whole wheat flour, all-purpose flour, salt, and cinnamon in a large bowl.

Add the yeast and honey to the bowl of the stand mixer and mix with a silicone spatula until combined. Add the melted butter and half of the flour mixture and mix until just combined and no large streaks of flour remain. Add the remaining flour and raisins. Attach the bowl to the stand mixer fitted with the dough hook. Mix on low speed just until the dough comes together, stopping the mixer to scrape down the bowl as necessary. Increase the speed to medium and mix until the dough forms a ball and pulls away from the sides of the bowl.

Pour the olive oil into a large bowl. Transfer the dough to the bowl and turn it to coat it in the oil. Cover with a clean kitchen towel and let rise in a warm place until doubled in size, at least 1 hour.

Lightly spray a 9 × 5-inch loaf pan with cooking spray.

Lightly flour a clean work surface, your hands, and a rolling pin. Punch the dough down once to release some of the air bubbles. Transfer the dough to the floured work surface and gently roll it out into a 9 × 15-inch rectangle. Starting with one short end, roll the dough up like you would a jelly roll, gently tucking in the ends. Transfer the dough, seam side down, to the prepared pan. Cover with a kitchen towel and let rise until it's risen above the edge of the loaf pan, about 1 hour.

Preheat the oven to 375°F.

Whisk the egg with a splash of water in a small bowl. Use a pastry brush to coat the top of the loaf with the egg wash. Bake for 40 to 50 minutes, until the crust is lightly golden.

Let the bread cool in the pan for 15 minutes before transferring it to a wire rack to cool completely before slicing.

Bertinelli Bread Dough

PHOTO ON PAGE 117

This recipe got my grandmother through every meal. I am sure generations of Bertinellis before her did the same, so I've named it after all the women in my family who didn't believe a meal was a meal unless there was a loaf of bread or a basket of rolls on the table. This recipe makes beautiful white bread and out-of-this-world dinner rolls. Try it for hamburger buns, too.

6 cups all-purpose flour, plus more for dusting

One ¼-ounce packet instant yeast (2¼ teaspoons)

3 tablespoons sugar

2 teaspoons kosher salt

2 cups lukewarm water (about 105°F)

5 tablespoons unsalted butter, melted and cooled to room temperature

1 tablespoon extra virgin olive oil

For the Rolls

Cooking spray

6 tablespoons unsalted butter

Flaky sea salt or kosher salt, for sprinkling

For the Loaves

Cooking spray

2 tablespoons unsalted butter

For the Buns

1 large egg

Sesame seeds (optional)

Whisk together 3 cups of the flour, the yeast, sugar, and salt in the bowl of a stand mixer. Pour in the water and use a silicone spatula to mix until the ingredients are evenly combined. Add the melted butter and the remaining 3 cups flour and mix again until a very shaggy dough forms. Attach the bowl to the stand mixer fitted with the dough hook. Mix on medium-low speed, stopping the mixer to scrape down the bowl as necessary, until the dough has pulled away from the sides of the bowl and is elastic and soft to the touch, 5 to 7 minutes.

Pour the olive oil into a large bowl. Transfer the dough to the bowl and turn it to coat it in the oil. Cover with a clean kitchen towel and let rise in a warm place until doubled in size, at least 1 hour.

TURN THE DOUGH INTO DINNER ROLLS

Spray a 9 × 13-inch baking dish with cooking spray. Lightly flour a clean work surface and your hands.

Punch the dough down once to release some of the air bubbles. Transfer the dough to the floured work surface. Cut the dough into sixteen equal portions and form into balls. Transfer the dough balls seam side down to the prepared baking dish. Cover with a clean kitchen towel and let sit until puffed, 1 hour.

Preheat the oven to 375°F.

Melt 6 tablespoons of unsalted butter. Use a pastry brush to gently brush the tops of the dinner rolls with half of the melted butter. Bake for 25 to 30 minutes, until golden brown. Brush with the remaining melted butter. Sprinkle with flaky sea salt or kosher salt. Serve warm.

TURN THE DOUGH INTO LOAVES

Spray two 8½ × 4½-inch loaf pans with cooking spray. Lightly flour a clean work surface, a rolling pin, and your hands.

Punch the dough down once to release some of the air bubbles. Transfer the dough to the floured work surface and cut into two equal portions. Working with half of the dough at a time, roll the dough into a 5 × 10-inch rectangle. Starting at one short end, roll the dough up like a jelly roll. Transfer the roll, seam side down, to one of the prepared loaf pans. Repeat with the other half of the dough. Cover both loaf pans with a clean kitchen towel and let rise until the center dome of the dough has risen over the edges of the loaf pan, about 1 hour.

Preheat the oven to 375°F. Melt 2 tablespoons of unsalted butter.

Use a pastry brush to gently brush the loaves with the butter. Bake for 35 to 45 minutes, until golden on top. Let cool for 10 minutes in the pans before transferring to a wire rack to cool completely.

TURN THE DOUGH INTO BUNS

Line a baking sheet with parchment paper. Lightly flour a clean work surface and your hands.

Punch the dough down once to release some of the air bubbles. Transfer the dough to the floured work surface. Cut the dough into eight equal portions and form into balls. Transfer the dough balls seam side down to the prepared baking sheet. Flatten each dough ball slightly so it's about 4 inches in diameter. Cover with a clean kitchen towel and let sit until puffed, 30 minutes.

Preheat the oven to 375°F.

Whisk an egg with a splash of water in a small bowl. Use a pastry brush to gently brush the tops and sides of the buns with the egg wash. Sprinkle each bun with a pinch or more of sesame seeds if you like! Bake for 25 to 30 minutes, until golden brown. Let cool to room temperature.

Chive Popovers

Popovers are the American version of the English classic Yorkshire pudding. They hold their shape yet seem as if they might float away. They are light, savory, chewy, and adaptable—you can serve them for breakfast, lunch, or dinner. They take butter and jam as easily as they do gravy and meat. You don't have to tell your family and friends how easy they are to make.

¼ cup beef drippings, bacon fat, or neutral oil (such as vegetable oil, avocado oil, or grapeseed oil)

2 large eggs

¾ cup all-purpose flour

¾ cup milk

½ teaspoon kosher salt

¼ teaspoon freshly ground black pepper

2 tablespoons chopped chives

Preheat the oven to 425°F. Divide the fat (drippings or oil) evenly among the cups of a 12-cup muffin tin (about 1 teaspoon per cup). Once the oven has preheated, transfer the pan to the oven to heat while you prepare the batter.

Whisk the eggs in a 32-ounce liquid measuring cup. Add the flour, milk, ½ cup of water, the salt, and pepper and whisk until smooth. There should be no lumps of flour remaining. The batter will be thin, which creates a light and fluffy popover.

Check on the muffin tin; you want the oil to be very hot and very lightly smoking. Remove the muffin tin from the oven and, working quickly to retain the heat of the pan, pour the batter evenly into the wells of the muffin tin. Divide the chives evenly over the batter. Transfer to the oven and bake for 25 minutes. Resist the urge to open the oven door to check on them, as this could cause the popovers to deflate.

Using an offset spatula, gently and carefully (the pan will be hot) remove the popovers from the pan. Transfer to a serving platter and serve immediately.

Multigrain Seeded Bread

The seeds give this bread a pleasant, chewy taste, intensifying the flavor, but I think the nuts are the crunchy highlight. This bread can be used to make any of the sandwiches in this book. If you have any slices left after a few days, try making a sumptuous grilled cheese sandwich. I speak from experience.

½ cup old-fashioned
rolled oats

1¾ cups boiling water

1¼ cups whole wheat flour

2 cups all-purpose flour, plus
more for dusting

1½ teaspoons kosher salt

1 tablespoon flaxseeds

2 tablespoons shelled
sunflower seeds

2 tablespoons sesame seeds

2 tablespoons raw pepitas

One ¼-ounce packet instant
yeast (2¼ teaspoons)

2 tablespoons honey

3 tablespoons unsalted
butter, melted and cooled
to room temperature

1 tablespoon extra virgin
olive oil

Cooking spray

1 large egg

Place the oats in the bowl of a stand mixer and cover with the boiling water. Let sit until the water reaches 105°F on an instant-read thermometer, 20 to 30 minutes.

Whisk together the whole wheat flour, all-purpose flour, and salt in a large bowl. In a separate small bowl, mix together the flaxseeds, sunflower seeds, sesame seeds, and pepitas.

Add the yeast and honey to the bowl of the stand mixer and mix with a silicone spatula until combined. Add the melted butter and half of the flour mixture and mix until just combined and no large streaks of flour remain. Add the remaining flour and attach the bowl to the stand mixer fitted with the dough hook. Mix on low speed just until the dough comes together, stopping the mixer to scrape down the bowl as necessary. Add 3 tablespoons of the seed mixture and increase the speed to medium. Continue to mix until the seeds are evenly incorporated and no loose seeds remain at the bottom of the bowl.

Pour the olive oil into a large bowl. Transfer the dough to the bowl and gently turn it to coat it in the oil. Cover with a clean kitchen towel and let rise in a warm place until doubled in size, at least 1 hour.

Lightly spray a 9 × 5-inch loaf pan with cooking spray and sprinkle 2 tablespoons of the seed mixture to lightly cover the bottom and sides of the pan. It won't cover it completely—that's okay!

Whisk the egg with a splash of water in a small bowl. Lightly flour a clean work surface, your hands, and a rolling pin. Punch the dough down once to release some of the air bubbles. Transfer the dough to the floured work surface and gently roll it into a 9 × 15-inch rectangle. Starting with one short end, roll the dough up like you would a jelly roll, gently tucking in the ends.

Transfer the dough, seam side down, to the prepared pan. Brush the top of the loaf with the egg wash and top with the remaining 1 tablespoon seed mix. Lightly press the seeds onto the dough to adhere. Cover with a kitchen towel and let rise until it's risen above the edge of the loaf pan, about 1 hour.

Preheat the oven to 375°F.

Bake for 40 to 50 minutes, until the crust is lightly golden. If the seeds begin to brown too much, you can tent the loaf with foil.

Let the bread cool in the pan for 15 minutes before transferring it to a wire rack to cool completely before slicing.

Milk Bread

Excellent for sandwiches or your morning toast, this is an easy-to-make and delicious bread for novice bakers and all those who have been too scared to make bread. What's the old line? *Try it, you'll like it*—especially that sense of accomplishment and the aroma that will fill your kitchen. There is nothing like a sandwich made with a couple of slices of fresh bread straight from the oven.

Cooking spray

1 tablespoon cornmeal

3 cups bread flour, plus more for dusting

2 teaspoons sugar

1 teaspoon kosher salt

¼ teaspoon baking soda

Two ¼-ounce packets instant yeast (4½ teaspoons)

1½ cups milk

2 tablespoons unsalted butter

Spray a 9 × 5-inch loaf pan with cooking spray and sprinkle the cornmeal all over the inside of the pan. Tap out any excess.

Whisk together the flour, sugar, salt, baking soda, and yeast in a large bowl. Set aside.

Combine the milk and butter in a small saucepan. Attach a candy thermometer and bring the mixture to 125°F over low heat. If the mixture gets too hot, let it cool to the correct temperature before continuing.

Pour the warm milk mixture over the dry ingredients and use a silicone spatula to mix until the dough comes together but is still shaggy. Turn the dough out onto a lightly floured work surface and knead until the dough is soft and elastic, 2 to 3 minutes. Form the dough into a log and transfer it seam side down to the prepared loaf pan. Cover with a clean kitchen towel and let rise in a warm place until it's puffed up and almost doubled in size, about 1 hour.

While the dough is rising, preheat the oven to 400°F.

Bake for 25 to 30 minutes, until the top of the bread is golden and the internal temperature reaches 190°F on an instant-read thermometer. Let cool in the pan for 10 minutes, then transfer to a wire rack to cool completely before slicing.

Pretzel Buns

The chewy exterior. The crunch of flaky sea salt. The fluffy, soft inside. Are you drooling yet? I got such a good reaction after I made these on *Valerie's Home Cooking*. People said they were as simple and delicious as I promised. Whether you serve a warm basket of these straight out of the oven or turn them into a sandwich (see Ham and Brie Sandwiches on Pretzel Buns on page 36), these buns are going to earn you major accolades. Just shrug and say, "'Twas nothing. Valerie told me to indulge."

For the Dough

1½ cups lukewarm water (about 105°F)

One ¼-ounce packet active dry yeast (2¼ teaspoons)

1 teaspoon kosher salt

½ stick (4 tablespoons) unsalted butter, melted and cooled to room temperature

3¼ cups unbleached all-purpose flour, plus more for dusting

Flaky sea salt, for sprinkling

For the Water Bath

½ cup baking soda

To make the dough, combine the water and yeast in a large bowl and allow the yeast to bloom for 5 minutes. Whisk in the kosher salt and 1 tablespoon of the melted butter. Add the flour and stir until the dough is shaggy but mostly holds together.

Lightly flour a clean work surface and your hands. Transfer the dough to the lightly floured surface and knead until springy, not sticky, about 3 minutes, adding more flour as needed to prevent sticking. Form the dough into a ball and place it back in the bowl. Cover and let rise in a warm place until the dough has doubled in size, about 1 hour.

Punch the dough down once to release some of the air bubbles. Turn the dough out onto the lightly floured surface and, with a pizza cutter or a sharp knife, divide the dough into eight equal pieces. Form each piece into a ball and place seam side down on a cutting board. Let rise, uncovered, for 10 minutes.

Preheat the oven to 400°F. Line a baking sheet with parchment paper.

To make the water bath, in a large pot bring the baking soda and 12 cups of water to a light simmer over low to medium heat.

Once the water is simmering, using a slotted spoon, transfer the dough balls, two to three at a time, into the water. Let them sit in the water for 20 seconds, flipping halfway through. Carefully remove each bun, making sure to drain off as much liquid as possible, and place on the prepared baking sheet. Repeat with the remaining buns.

Using a sharp knife, make an X on the top of each bun. Brush the buns with the remaining 3 tablespoons melted butter and sprinkle with a generous pinch of flaky salt. Bake for 25 minutes, or until golden brown. Let cool for 10 to 15 minutes before slicing.

Cook's Note

If not using all the buns immediately, freeze in a zip-top bag. To reheat, warm in a 350°F oven for 10 minutes.

White Bean
and Kale Soup

(page 147)

SOUPS

"You don't just taste a good soup; you feel it from head to toe. It fills your heart and belly like no other food."

Chicken Chili with Poblanos and Corn

You'll have to decide whether this dish is chili or soup. I don't think it matters. As a chili, it's terrific, but I think it has the texture of a soup. I particularly love the sweet crunch of the corn and the smokiness of the poblanos.

2 tablespoons vegetable oil

1½ pounds boneless, skinless chicken thighs

Kosher salt and freshly ground black pepper

1 yellow onion, diced

2 poblano peppers, seeded and diced

1 red bell pepper, diced

5 garlic cloves, minced

1 zucchini, quartered and sliced

1 teaspoon ground cumin

1 teaspoon chili powder

¼ teaspoon cayenne pepper

4 cups low-sodium chicken stock

¼ cup coarse cornmeal

1½ cups fresh sweet corn (from 3 ears)

One 15-ounce can white beans (navy, great northern, or cannellini), drained and rinsed

Assorted toppings (diced avocado, sour cream, sliced green onions, freshly grated Monterey Jack, cilantro leaves), for serving

Heat the vegetable oil in a large Dutch oven over medium-high heat. Pat the chicken dry and season both sides well with salt and pepper. Transfer the chicken to the Dutch oven and cook until it easily releases from the pan and is golden brown, 5 to 7 minutes. Flip and cook for an additional 2 minutes. Transfer to a plate and set aside. The chicken does not need to be fully cooked at this point; it will continue to cook later.

If the pan looks dry, add another tablespoon of oil. Add the onion, poblanos, bell pepper, and ½ teaspoon salt to the Dutch oven and sauté until the vegetables are softened and the onion is translucent, about 5 minutes. Add the garlic and zucchini and cook for an additional 2 minutes. Add the cumin, chili powder, and cayenne and stir to coat the vegetables in the spices. Add the stock and chicken thighs, bring the mixture to a boil, then reduce the heat to low, cover, and simmer until the chicken is fully cooked and shreds easily, about 20 minutes.

Transfer the chicken to a plate. Add the cornmeal, corn, and beans to the Dutch oven and stir to combine. Use two forks to shred the chicken into bite-size pieces. Return the chicken and any accumulated juices to the Dutch oven and simmer until the chili is slightly thickened, about 5 minutes. Season to taste with salt and pepper. Ladle into bowls and serve with desired toppings.

Ginger Turmeric Bone Broth

I love this simple and delicious broth. Sometimes I freeze individual portions and have a cup at night instead of my usual chamomile tea. It hits the spot, especially on a chilly evening when I'm reading a book in front of the fireplace.

1 whole cooked chicken carcass (meat reserved for another use)

1 yellow onion, peeled and quartered

2 carrots, halved

2 celery stalks, halved

6 garlic cloves, smashed

One 3-inch piece of ginger, sliced

2 small knobs fresh turmeric, halved

1 teaspoon black peppercorns

2 tablespoons apple cider vinegar

2 bay leaves

Kosher salt

Filtered water

Place the chicken carcass, onion, carrots, celery, garlic, ginger, turmeric, peppercorns, vinegar, bay leaves, and 1 teaspoon of salt in a large Dutch oven. Add enough filtered water to cover everything, about 12 cups. Bring to a boil over high heat, then reduce to a low simmer and cook, stirring occasionally, for 4 hours.

Strain the broth through a fine-mesh strainer or cheesecloth and season to taste with salt. Discard the carcass and vegetables. Pour the broth into quart jars or airtight containers. Let cool completely before covering and refrigerating.

After the broth has been refrigerated, the fat will rise to the top and solidify. Remove the fat with a spoon and paper towel before using.

Store in an airtight container in the fridge for up to 5 days and in the freezer for up to 10 months.

Loaded Miso Soup

The Japanese term "umami" refers to the "core of deliciousness," and I believe that perfectly captures the essence of miso. I usually have a little carton of this versatile ingredient in my refrigerator for those moments when I crave a light but flavorful meal. This soup is chock-full of wholesome ingredients, and it hits the spot every time.

4 cups vegetable broth

3 tablespoons white or yellow miso paste

2 tablespoons grated ginger

3 garlic cloves, grated

1 cup small broccoli florets

½ cup carrot matchsticks

1 cup thinly sliced cremini mushrooms

1 head baby bok choy, sliced

1 cup beech mushrooms, root ends removed

3 ounces enoki mushrooms, root ends removed

8 ounces firm tofu, cut into bite-size cubes

Sliced green onions, for garnish

Combine the broth, 2 cups of water, the miso paste, ginger, and garlic in a Dutch oven or large pot. Bring to a boil over medium-high heat, whisking occasionally to mix the miso paste into the broth.

Add the broccoli, carrots, and cremini mushrooms. Stir to combine, reduce the heat to a simmer, and cook until the vegetables are tender, about 5 minutes.

Next, add the bok choy, beech mushrooms, enoki mushrooms, and tofu. Cook until the mushrooms are soft and the tofu is heated through, an additional 5 minutes.

Ladle into bowls and garnish with green onions.

Quick Turkey and Butternut Squash Soup

Wolfie had just come off tour and asked me to bring some turkey meatball soup to his house. I didn't have time to make the meatballs, but I still wanted to give him all the flavors he remembered as a child—plus some extra nutrients to help him recover, since life on the road can be hard. Luckily, I had a butternut squash on hand. The soup was so good I just had to share it.

3 slices thick-cut bacon, chopped

1 medium yellow onion, diced

1 pound ground dark meat turkey

Kosher salt and freshly ground black pepper

1 large leek, dark green part discarded, light green and white part halved, sliced, and cleaned

2 celery stalks, chopped

3 cups cubed butternut squash

7 cups low-sodium chicken stock

1 large Parmesan rind

4 cups roughly chopped curly kale

Heat a large Dutch oven over medium-high heat. Add the bacon and cook, stirring occasionally, until the fat begins to render and the bacon crisps up, about 3 minutes.

Add the onion to the pot and stir to combine. Cook until the onion softens slightly, 2 to 3 minutes. Next, add the turkey and season with a generous pinch of salt and pepper. Cook, breaking up the turkey into bite-size pieces, until no pink remains, about 4 minutes.

Add the leek and celery to the pot and cook until lightly softened, 3 to 4 minutes. Next, add the butternut squash, chicken stock, and Parmesan rind and bring to a boil. Reduce the heat to low, cover, and simmer until the butternut squash has cooked through, 15 minutes. Remove and discard the Parmesan rind.

Stir in the kale to submerge it into the soup. Cook until the kale is wilted and softened, about 3 minutes. Season to taste with salt and pepper.

Cook's Note

You can freeze this soup for up to 3 months. Just let it cool completely before transferring it to a freezer-safe container.

Roasted Cauliflower and Garlic Soup

This delicious creamy soup does not have a drop of cream in it. The potatoes and cauliflower blend together and take on all the rich flavors of the garlic and thyme to become something really very special. Indulge again and again.

1 head cauliflower, cut into 2-inch pieces (about 8 cups)

20 garlic cloves, peeled

¼ cup plus 2 tablespoons extra virgin olive oil

Kosher salt and freshly ground black pepper

1 pound russet potatoes, cut into ½-inch chunks

1 yellow onion, diced

2 celery stalks, chopped

1 tablespoon thyme leaves

½ cup white wine

6 cups low-sodium chicken stock

6-ounce Parmigiano-Reggiano rind

Freshly grated Parmigiano-Reggiano, for serving

Preheat the oven to 400°F.

Place the cauliflower and garlic on a baking sheet. Drizzle with ¼ cup of the olive oil and season generously with salt and pepper. Toss to coat. Roast for 25 minutes, until the cauliflower is fork-tender and lightly charred in places.

Heat a Dutch oven over medium-high heat. Add the remaining 2 tablespoons olive oil, the potatoes, onion, celery, and thyme. Season with a generous pinch of salt and pepper. Cook, stirring often, until the vegetables have softened slightly, about 5 minutes. Pour in the wine to deglaze the pan, scraping up any browned bits from the bottom of the pan. Add the roasted cauliflower and garlic, stock, and cheese rind. Bring to a boil, then reduce the heat to low and cover. Simmer, stirring occasionally to prevent the cheese rind from sticking to the bottom of the pan, for 25 minutes. Remove and discard the cheese rind.

Working in batches so as not to overfill the blender, carefully transfer the mixture to a high-powered blender. Place the lid on the blender, leaving one corner open to release the heat. Cover the lid with a kitchen towel to catch any splatters and blend (starting on low and gradually increasing to medium-high) until completely smooth. Once all the soup is blended, return it to the Dutch oven and season to taste with salt and pepper. Ladle into bowls and garnish with a pinch of pepper and a sprinkle of Parmigiano-Reggiano.

Roasted Tomato Soup with Garlic Bread Croutons

I feel like I have to put a little spin on tomato soup in every cookbook simply because I freaking love tomato soup. So I'm indulging myself again. This one is all about the garlic bread croutons. The two are such a delicious combination.

For the Roasted Tomato Soup

3 pounds ripe tomatoes (a mix of vine-ripened, Roma, Campari, cherry, or whatever you may have on hand)

2 shallots, halved

10 garlic cloves, peeled

1 red bell pepper, chopped

⅓ cup extra virgin olive oil

Kosher salt and freshly ground black pepper

½ cup basil leaves

2 cups low-sodium chicken stock

½ cup heavy cream

1 teaspoon sugar (optional)

For the Garlic Bread Croutons

2 tablespoons roughly chopped parsley

2 tablespoons roughly chopped basil

2 garlic cloves

¼ teaspoon kosher salt

Preheat the oven to 400°F. Line a baking sheet with parchment paper.

To make the soup, cut any larger tomatoes in half (leave cherry tomatoes whole) and place them on the prepared baking sheet along with the shallots, garlic, and bell pepper. Drizzle with the olive oil and season generously with salt and pepper. Toss to coat.

Roast for 40 minutes, until the tomatoes are soft and beginning to brown in places. Remove from the oven and let cool for 10 minutes. Leave the oven on to make the croutons.

Working in batches, transfer the roasted vegetables to a high-powered blender. Fill the blender halfway with the first batch. Add the basil and place the lid on the blender, leaving one corner open to release the heat. Cover the lid with a kitchen towel to catch any splatters and blend (starting on low and gradually increasing to medium-high) until completely smooth. Transfer to a Dutch oven. Repeat with the remaining vegetables. Pour the stock into the pot and stir to combine. Bring the mixture to a boil over high heat, reduce the heat to a simmer, cover, and cook for 10 minutes.

Stir in the cream and sugar (if using). Season to taste with salt and pepper. Keep warm until ready to serve.

To make the croutons, combine the parsley, basil, garlic, and salt in a small food processor and pulse until the mixture is

recipe continues

5 tablespoons unsalted
butter, room temperature

2 tablespoons freshly grated
Parmesan

½ baguette, sliced in half
lengthwise

finely chopped. Add the butter and Parmesan and pulse to fully incorporate.

Arrange the baguette on a clean work surface. Spread the butter mixture evenly on both of the cut sides. Sandwich the two halves together and wrap in foil. Place on a baking sheet and bake for 10 minutes.

Remove the baking sheet from the oven and turn the broiler to high. Carefully unwrap the foil and lay flat on the baking sheet. Open the bread to expose the butter sides. Return the baking sheet to the oven and broil until the edges are toasted, about 1 minute. Keep an eye on the bread; the browning can happen fast and every broiler is a little different. Cut the croutons into 1- to 2-inch cubes.

To serve, ladle the soup into bowls and top with croutons.

White Bean and Kale Soup

PHOTO ON PAGE 132

This simplified version of a traditional Tuscan family meal loses nothing in translation. The white beans and kale pair perfectly and absorb all the flavors. The longer it simmers, the better it tastes.

1 tablespoon extra virgin olive oil, plus more for serving

1 yellow onion, diced

2 celery stalks, diced

2 medium carrots, diced

Kosher salt and freshly ground black pepper

¼ cup celery leaves, chopped

4 garlic cloves, grated

1 teaspoon finely chopped rosemary

6 cups low-sodium chicken stock

Three 15-ounce cans cannellini beans, drained and rinsed

1 small bunch lacinato kale, ribs removed, roughly chopped (3 to 4 cups)

Freshly grated Parmesan, for serving

Heat the olive oil in a Dutch oven over medium-high heat. Add the onion, celery, and carrots and season with salt and pepper. Cook, stirring occasionally, until the onion is translucent and the carrots have softened, about 7 minutes. Add the celery leaves, garlic, and rosemary and cook until the garlic is fragrant, about 1 minute.

Pour the broth and beans into the pot and season with salt and pepper. Bring to a boil over high heat, then reduce the heat to low and simmer for 10 minutes.

Use a ladle to carefully transfer one-third of the soup to a high-powered blender. Place the lid on the blender, leaving one corner open to release the heat. Cover the lid with a kitchen towel to catch any splatters and blend (starting on low and gradually increasing to medium-high) until completely smooth. Transfer the blended mixture back to the pot and stir to combine.

Bring the soup back to a boil over medium-high heat. Add the kale and cook until it's bright and wilted, 2 to 3 minutes. Remove from the heat and season to taste with salt and pepper.

To serve, ladle the soup into bowls. Top with Parmesan, more pepper, and a drizzle of olive oil.

Roasted
Cabbage

(page 163)

VEGETABLES

"I love browsing my local farmers' market. I touch and taste and ask questions. I marvel at all the different shapes, sizes, and colors. The imperfections on the outside intrigue me. I know the tasty, good stuff is on the inside. All I see is possibility."

Baby Kale with Crispy Garlic

I don't think baby kale has enjoyed the breakthrough it deserves. No slicing, no massaging—just indulge in these cute little mini kale leaves. This side dish is super easy to whip up. I particularly love it with grilled rib eye. Whatever I don't eat gets mixed with scrambled eggs the next morning.

2 tablespoons extra virgin olive oil

5 garlic cloves, thinly sliced

10 ounces baby kale

Kosher salt and freshly ground black pepper

1 tablespoon lemon juice

Add the olive oil and garlic to a cold pan. Turn the heat to medium and cook until the garlic is lightly golden and crisp, 3 to 4 minutes. Use a slotted spoon to transfer the garlic to a paper towel–lined plate and set aside.

Increase the heat to medium-high and add the kale to the pan. Season with a pinch of salt and pepper and stir to combine. Cook, stirring frequently, until the kale is wilted and bright green, about 2 minutes. Remove from the heat and add the lemon juice. Season to taste with salt and pepper.

Transfer the kale to a serving bowl and top with the crispy garlic.

Blistered Green Beans

I have a confession: green beans have never been on my list of favorites. But blistering them in this manner makes me love them, and the rice vinegar and grated ginger give them an intense flavor that I find irresistible.

2 tablespoons low-sodium
   soy sauce

1 teaspoon rice vinegar

2 teaspoons grated ginger

3 garlic cloves, grated

2 tablespoons avocado oil

1 pound green
   beans, trimmed

Kosher salt

Whisk together the soy sauce, rice vinegar, ginger, and garlic in a small bowl.

Heat the avocado oil in a wok or large high-sided pan over medium-high heat. Once the oil is shimmering, add the green beans and toss to coat them in the oil. Season with a pinch of salt. Spread them out in as even a layer as possible and cook, undisturbed, until they begin to blister and char, 3 to 4 minutes. Keep cooking, tossing occasionally, until the beans are evenly blistered and soft, another 3 to 5 minutes. Transfer the beans to a plate.

Add the sauce to the pan and cook while stirring until the garlic is fragrant, about 30 seconds. Return the beans to the pan and toss to coat them in the sauce.

Transfer to a serving platter and serve immediately.

Charred Asparagus

Along with broccoli, asparagus is my favorite vegetable. Charred with a little olive oil, salt, and pepper, it becomes a flavorsome delicacy. I pick up the spears and eat them like fries. Drizzling the asparagus with Bagna Cauda takes this to a whole other level of indulgence.

1 bunch thick-stem asparagus, trimmed

1 tablespoon extra virgin olive oil

½ teaspoon kosher salt

¼ teaspoon freshly ground black pepper

2 tablespoons Bagna Cauda (page 52)

1 lemon

¼ cup smoked almonds, chopped

1 teaspoon chopped oregano

Preheat the oven to broil. Line a baking sheet with foil.

Place the asparagus on the prepared baking sheet. Drizzle with the olive oil and season with the salt and pepper. Toss to coat. Broil for 3 to 4 minutes, until the asparagus begins to char. (Everyone's broiler is slightly different, so be sure to keep an eye on the asparagus.) Remove the baking sheet from the oven and toss the asparagus. Return to the broiler for another few minutes, until the asparagus is bright green and charred in places.

To serve, transfer the asparagus to a serving platter and drizzle with the bagna cauda. Use a fine zester to zest the lemon over the asparagus. Cut the lemon in half and squeeze the juice of half the lemon over the asparagus. Top with smoked almonds and chopped oregano. Serve immediately.

Cold Miso Peanut Zoodles

If you have a spiralizer, you can make zoodles—zucchini noodles. They are a great, veggie-forward alternative to pasta and I can't recommend them enough. Wolfie's wife, Andraia, loves when I make shrimp scampi with zoodles, and I also do zoodles and Bolognese. But these cold miso peanut zoodles are my favorite. Make sure you don't overcook them, as they taste best when they're crunchy.

2 teaspoons coconut oil

2 large zucchini, spiralized
(about 5 cups)

1 large carrot, grated
(about 1 cup)

½ teaspoon kosher salt

¼ cup Ginger Miso Dressing
(page 326)

1 tablespoon creamy peanut
butter (page 310 or
store-bought)

½ teaspoon Sambal Oelek
(page 328 or store-bought;
optional)

½ teaspoon toasted
sesame oil

2 tablespoons chopped
cilantro, plus whole leaves
for garnish

2 green onions, sliced
(reserve 1 tablespoon for
garnish)

Black sesame seeds,
for garnish

Crushed peanuts, for garnish

Line a baking sheet with paper towels.

Melt the coconut oil in a large nonstick skillet over medium-high heat. Add the zucchini, carrot, and salt and cook, stirring frequently, until the zucchini is just beginning to soften and turn bright green, about 3 minutes. Remove from the heat and transfer the veggies to the prepared baking sheet. Spread them out in an even layer and let cool.

Whisk together the miso dressing, peanut butter, sambal oelek (if using), and sesame oil in a large bowl.

Add the zucchini mixture, chopped cilantro, and green onions to the bowl with the dressing and toss to combine.

To serve, divide the zoodles evenly between two bowls. Top with cilantro leaves, reserved green onions, black sesame seeds, and crushed peanuts.

Glazed Sweet Potatoes

Years ago, after reading about the nutritional benefits of sweet potatoes (high fiber and antioxidants), I started ordering them whenever they were on a menu. Then I figured out different ways to make them myself. This is my new favorite. The little bit of soy sauce and rice vinegar balances the sweetness of the turmeric ginger honey glaze; it's delish.

5 tablespoons
   unsalted butter

3 small sweet potatoes (about
   1½ pounds)

¼ cup Turmeric Ginger Honey
   (page 311)

3 tablespoons low-sodium
   soy sauce

1 tablespoon rice vinegar

Toasted sesame seeds,
   for garnish

Preheat the oven to 375°F. Grease a 9 × 13-inch baking dish with 1 tablespoon of the butter.

Cut each sweet potato into eight wedges and place them in an even layer in the prepared baking dish. Set aside.

Melt the remaining 4 tablespoons butter in a small saucepan over medium heat. Add the honey, soy sauce, and rice vinegar. Stir to combine and remove from the heat.

Pour the butter mixture over the sweet potatoes and toss to coat. Cover the baking dish with foil and roast for 45 minutes to 1 hour, until the sweet potatoes are tender but still hold their shape.

Carefully transfer the sweet potatoes to a serving dish. Spoon the glaze over the potatoes and garnish with sesame seeds.

Ratatouille

I ordered ratatouille for the first time in the early 1980s, when I was a regular at a chic little café in West Hollywood. All these years later, I love to indulge in this French classic when my farmers' market is full of fresh veggies. Eat with nice crusty bread, wrap some in a tortilla, or mix with scrambled eggs. There are so many ways to devour this delicious dish.

¼ cup extra virgin olive oil

1 medium eggplant, cut into ½- to 1-inch pieces (4 to 5 cups)

Kosher salt and freshly ground black pepper

1 yellow onion, diced

1 red bell pepper, diced

1 yellow bell pepper, diced

5 garlic cloves, grated

1 medium zucchini, cut into ½- to 1-inch pieces

1 yellow squash, cut into ½- to 1-inch pieces

1 cup cherry tomatoes, halved

One 14-ounce can crushed tomatoes

1 teaspoon lemon zest

1 tablespoon chopped oregano

¼ cup chopped basil

1 tablespoon freshly squeezed lemon juice

Pesto (page 336 or store-bought), for serving (optional)

Heat 2 tablespoons of the olive oil in a large Dutch oven over medium heat. Once the oil is shimmering, add the eggplant and season with ½ teaspoon salt and ¼ teaspoon pepper. Cook, stirring occasionally, until the eggplant is evenly browned and soft, about 10 minutes. Transfer to a plate and set aside.

Add the remaining 2 tablespoons olive oil to the Dutch oven. Add the onion and bell peppers and season with ½ teaspoon salt and ¼ teaspoon pepper. Cook, stirring occasionally, until the vegetables begin to soften, about 4 minutes. Add the garlic, zucchini, yellow squash, and cherry tomatoes and season with ½ teaspoon salt and ¼ teaspoon pepper. Cook, stirring occasionally, until the squash begins to soften and the tomatoes begin to release their juices but still hold their shape, about 5 minutes. Add the crushed tomatoes, lemon zest, oregano, and basil and stir to combine. Bring the mixture to a simmer, then reduce the heat to low and stir the eggplant back in. Cook, stirring occasionally, until the vegetables are soft but still hold their shape, 20 to 30 minutes.

Remove from the heat and stir in the lemon juice. Season to taste with salt and pepper.

To serve, spoon ratatouille into bowls and top with a drizzle of pesto, if using.

Roasted Cabbage

You may be asking, "Is she serious? Roasted cabbage?" Yes, I'm serious. Roasted, seasoned, and drizzled with my Dill Pickle Vinaigrette, this cabbage is equivalent to Cinderella trying on a glass slipper. The perfect fit for this underappreciated veggie. The transformation is wonderful. So much flavor is pulled out. And the wedges look elegant on the plate.

1 medium head
   green cabbage

½ cup Dill Pickle Vinaigrette
   (page 327)

Kosher salt and freshly
   ground black pepper

1 to 2 tablespoons Easy Garlic
   Chili Crisp (page 330 or
   store-bought chili crisp)

Dill fronds, for garnish

Preheat the oven to 450°F. Line a baking sheet with parchment paper.

Trim any discoloration from the root of the cabbage and remove any soft or discolored outer leaves. Carefully cut the cabbage into six wedges, being sure to keep the root intact so the wedge stays together. Place the wedges in a large bowl and drizzle with the dressing. Being careful to keep the wedges intact, gently toss the cabbage in the dressing, coating it completely.

Place the wedges on the prepared baking sheet and season with salt and pepper. Roast for 25 to 30 minutes, flipping after 15 minutes. The cabbage should be soft and charred.

Transfer the wedges to a serving platter and drizzle with your desired amount of chili crisp and garnish with dill.

Savory Snap Peas and Mushrooms

I can picture myself sautéing snow peas and mushrooms on the little stove in the place I lived after moving out of my parents' house. I still love this combination, except now I use snap peas and add a garlic and soy sauce mixture for a little extra zing. One of my go-to dishes, it's full of freshness and flavor and simplicity.

2 garlic cloves, grated

2 tablespoons low-sodium soy sauce

1 tablespoon rice vinegar

½ teaspoon toasted sesame oil

2 tablespoons coconut oil

8 ounces cremini mushrooms, sliced

½ yellow onion, sliced

Kosher salt and freshly ground black pepper

10 ounces snap peas, trimmed

2 green onions, sliced, for garnish

Whisk together the garlic, soy sauce, rice vinegar, and sesame oil in a small bowl. Set aside.

Melt 1 tablespoon of the coconut oil in a large nonstick skillet over medium heat. Add the mushrooms, onion, and a pinch of salt and pepper. Cook, stirring occasionally, until the mushrooms have released their liquid and softened, 5 to 7 minutes.

Add the remaining 1 tablespoon coconut oil and the snap peas to the skillet with the mushrooms and onion. Season with a pinch of salt. Cook, stirring occasionally, until the snap peas are bright green and beginning to soften, about 3 minutes. Add the garlic and soy sauce mixture and cook until the snap peas are crisp-tender, 3 to 4 minutes.

Transfer the snap peas and mushrooms to a serving bowl and garnish with green onions.

Vegetable Galette

Whenever I have an abundance of vegetables, I think galette. I love a good one. The key is to take the time to arrange the vegetables beautifully. It will look gorgeous when you take it out of the oven. I guarantee your family and friends will be impressed, and rightfully so. But don't tell them how easy it is to make.

4 ounces goat cheese, room temperature

4 ounces ricotta

1 teaspoon lemon zest

½ teaspoon Italian seasoning

½ teaspoon garlic powder

½ teaspoon onion powder

Kosher salt and freshly ground black pepper

½ cup sliced zucchini (¼ inch thick)

½ cup sliced yellow squash (¼ inch thick)

½ cup multicolor cherry tomatoes, sliced

1 tablespoon extra virgin olive oil

1 store-bought pie crust dough

1 large egg

1 tablespoon freshly grated Parmesan

Chopped chives, for garnish

Preheat the oven to 375°F. Line a baking sheet with parchment paper.

Combine the goat cheese, ricotta, lemon zest, Italian seasoning, garlic powder, and onion powder in a small bowl. Season with a pinch of salt and pepper and mix until evenly combined. Set aside.

Combine the zucchini, yellow squash, and cherry tomatoes in a large bowl. Drizzle with the olive oil and season with ½ teaspoon salt and ¼ teaspoon pepper. Gently toss to coat. Set aside.

Unroll the pie dough on the prepared baking sheet. Add the goat cheese mixture to the center of the pie dough and spread it into an even layer, leaving a 2-inch border all the way around. Arrange the vegetables on top of the goat cheese mixture, layering and shingling them as necessary. Fold the crust around the edge of the filling, pleating as needed.

Whisk the egg with 1 tablespoon of water in a small bowl. Use a pastry brush to brush the egg wash on any exposed crust. Sprinkle the crust with the Parmesan.

Bake for 35 minutes, until the crust is golden brown and the vegetables are soft.

Let sit for 5 minutes before garnishing with chives and serving.

Dinner for One

I recently made one of my all-time favorite dishes for dinner—pasta vongole. I don't know how you decide what to make if you're dining alone, but let me tell you how I chose my menu.

I had been in Amsterdam to see my son and his band on tour. We were staying in the same hotel where his father and I had stayed before I got pregnant. Being back there was special for many reasons. Wolfie was thirty-one, engaged, and performing in front of thousands of people. It was amazing to see the way his confidence had grown since he had released his first album and formed his band a few years earlier. My favorite shows were when he was relaxed enough to reveal his sense of humor.

I don't know if I was the best mom in the world, but it is the role that gave me the most pleasure, and I felt that even more as I noted my kid had turned into a kind and sensitive and hardworking young man. Despite my many mistakes and challenges along the way, all the patience, laughter, and unconditional love seemed to have paid off. Just as butter and salt can save most recipes gone awry, love works the same magic on people. Got a problem? Add more love. Is someone upset? Pour some love on the situation.

On the spice rack of experience, another ingredient that helps is forgiveness. It had been on my mind because I had been finalizing my divorce from my second husband and quite a few people—some of whom I know, others I don't—had come up to me and said, "You need to forgive so you can move on."

But do I? I have felt like I can move on without forgiving right away. I've thought about forgiving the many things that led to that divorce, and I must admit, I'm having trouble doing that. I'm just not there yet, and I have found that trying to forgive before I'm ready is very stressful. I do know from raising my little rock and roller that forgiveness comes easily when you love someone. My relationship with Ed was the same way. Though we got divorced, Ed and I never stopped loving each other. Who knows, if not for cancer, we might have had a second wind.

I'm pretty sure that is wistful thinking. But the thought of my current situation crossed my mind as I flew home from Europe. As time passed, I surprised myself by doing okay without forgiving. I drank less, exercised more, and paid attention to what I put into my body. I felt my whole self—I finally sat with my emotions, no longer trying to numb or ignore them, but really doing my best to understand them. Not only did it make me feel good and strong, it began to help me put a positive spin on my attitude about the future.

A few days later, I was listening to the great blond philosopher of our time, music superstar Taylor Swift, being interviewed on TV, and I found myself nodding enthusiastically as she said it's easy to forgive someone when you know they give meaning and love to your life. And when they don't? I knew the answer from my own experience. When they don't, you must forgive yourself. Forgive the choices you made and the time you wasted.

You don't need to forgive everyone to move on. You can give yourself a break. Why did it take me so long to get to such a place of understanding? It doesn't matter. Everyone goes at their own speed.

By dinnertime, I was reveling in the peace that had come over me as I gave myself credit for indeed getting there with my son, my first husband, my parents, and most of all, myself. The peace I felt was good and satisfying, and as I got up to make myself dinner, I wanted something that would taste that same way: good and satisfying. You know what popped into my head? My childhood favorite, pasta vongole, which I used to order with my family at a roadside seafood diner when we lived in Delaware.

I checked my pantry and fridge. I had spaghetti on hand, also white wine, garlic, butter, olive oil, red pepper flakes . . . everything but the clams. A quick trip to the grocery store fixed that. The guy behind the seafood counter asked if I was celebrating anything special. I said, "Yes. Me!" "What's the occasion?" he asked. "Just had a good day," I said. The clams and broth took only a few minutes to prepare, and the pasta needed just a few minutes more before it was perfectly al dente. Then I sat down with a small salad, my beautifully plated pasta vongole, and a glass of cold water, and I let my meal take me back through sixty years of memories until I was a little girl in Delaware again, thinking nothing could ever be as delicious as each bite of that pasta vongole.

And that, my friends, is dinner for one—and who knows, maybe inspiration for a new Taylor Swift song.

Meal Prep
Grilled Chicken
Breasts

(page 191)

CHICKEN

"How many times have I heard people try something new and say, 'It tastes like chicken!' It's happened so often that I have decided almost everyone loves to eat chicken. Chicken dishes tend to be easy to make and difficult to botch. Just add enough flavor and you got it."

Chicken Breasts with Tomato Prosecco Sauce

I have specified using chicken breasts here, but I did that for the sake of variety because so many of my recipes call for thighs. Either is fine. I usually have a bottle of prosecco in the house, and while obviously the bubbles go away as it simmers, that little bit of sparkling wine adds a perky sweetness to the tomato sauce. It works, trust me. Cheers.

2 tablespoons unsalted butter, room temperature

2 tablespoons all-purpose flour

4 boneless, skinless chicken breasts

Kosher salt and freshly ground black pepper

Extra virgin olive oil

2 shallots, sliced into rings

2 cups cherry tomatoes, halved

1 cup rosé prosecco

½ cup low-sodium chicken stock

2 tablespoons drained capers

1 teaspoon lemon zest

3 garlic cloves, grated

Basil leaves, for garnish

Using a fork, mash the butter and flour together in a small bowl until evenly combined and no white spots of flour are visible. Set aside. This is called beurre manié and will help thicken the sauce similarly to a roux but with a lot less whisking!

Pat the chicken breasts dry. Transfer them to a zip-top bag or place between two pieces of plastic wrap and pound to an even thickness. Season both sides generously with salt and pepper.

Heat 2 tablespoons of olive oil in a large skillet over medium heat. Once the oil is shimmering, add the chicken breasts, smooth side down. You may need to work in batches to avoid crowding the pan. Cook until golden brown and crisp, 5 minutes. Flip and continue cooking for an additional 5 minutes. Transfer the chicken to a plate and set aside. Repeat with the remaining chicken, if you're cooking in batches. Feel free to add a bit more olive oil if the pan looks too dry between batches. The chicken does not need to be fully cooked at this point; it will continue to cook later.

Once all the chicken has been removed from the pan, add an additional 1 tablespoon of olive oil, then add the shallots and tomatoes. Season with ½ teaspoon salt and ¼ teaspoon pepper. Cook, stirring occasionally, until the tomatoes have released most of their juices and the shallots are softened.

Add the prosecco to deglaze the pan, scraping up any browned bits from the bottom of the pan. Cook until the harsh alcohol smell burns off and the liquid reduces slightly.

Add the stock, capers, lemon zest, and garlic. Bring the mixture to a boil, then reduce the heat to low and add the beurre manié, breaking it up into pieces as you add it to the pan. Whisk until it dissolves into the sauce. Cook until the sauce has thickened, about 3 minutes. Season to taste with salt and pepper.

Return the chicken to the pan and spoon some of the sauce over it. Cover and cook on low heat just until the chicken is fully cooked, 5 to 10 minutes.

Garnish with basil and serve.

Chicken Thigh Parm

Ordinarily, I would encourage you to keep the bone in and skin on your chicken thighs, to appreciate the flavor they bring to the party—and your palate. But with both the sauce and the cheese, there is plenty going on in this recipe to ensure every bite is packed with deliciousness. Boneless, skinless chicken thighs are also easier to cut into. No fingers are necessary for this one (unless you're mopping up the plate afterward).

½ teaspoon red pepper flakes

1 teaspoon Italian seasoning

½ teaspoon garlic powder

½ teaspoon onion powder

1 teaspoon kosher salt

¼ teaspoon freshly ground black pepper

4 boneless, skinless chicken thighs, pounded to an even thickness

2 tablespoons extra virgin olive oil

½ cup Marinara Sauce (page 335 or store-bought)

2 tablespoons chopped basil, plus whole leaves for garnish

1 cup freshly grated provolone (about 4 ounces)

2 tablespoons freshly grated Parmesan, plus more for garnish

Preheat the oven to 400°F. Line a baking sheet with parchment paper.

Stir together the pepper flakes, Italian seasoning, garlic powder, onion powder, salt, and black pepper in a small bowl until evenly combined. Season both sides of the chicken thighs with the seasoning mix.

Heat the olive oil in a large skillet over medium heat. Once the oil is shimmering, add the chicken thighs. You may need to work in batches to avoid crowding the pan. Cook until golden and crisp, 5 to 7 minutes. Flip and cook until golden on the other side, an additional 5 to 7 minutes. The chicken doesn't need to be fully cooked at this stage; it will continue to cook in the oven. Transfer the chicken to the prepared baking sheet.

Top the chicken evenly with the marinara sauce. Sprinkle with the chopped basil and top evenly with the provolone and Parmesan. Bake for 10 to 15 minutes, until the cheese is melted and lightly golden and the chicken is cooked through. Let cool for 5 minutes before serving. Top each thigh with Parmesan and basil leaves before serving.

Have Leftovers?

Cover the chicken with foil and reheat it in the oven at 325°F for 20 minutes, then serve it on toasted ciabatta with some extra sauce and basil.

Cornish Hens with Wild Rice Stuffing

Though my recipe for this dish has been considerably updated, perfected, and simplified, it goes back to when I was eighteen or nineteen and living on my own in my first house. Back then, I thought a little Cornish game hen was the fanciest dish to make and the surest way to impress dinner guests. All these years later, it's still impressive.

Extra virgin olive oil

1 sweet Italian sausage, casing removed

1 large shallot, finely diced

1 small carrot, finely diced

1 cup cremini mushrooms, finely diced

Kosher salt and freshly ground black pepper

½ cup finely diced Honeycrisp apple (from ½ apple)

¼ cup dried cranberries

3 garlic cloves, grated

¼ cup chopped walnuts

2 cups cooked wild rice blend

4 Cornish game hens

2 teaspoons Dijon mustard

Preheat the oven to 400°F. Line a baking sheet with parchment paper.

Heat 1 tablespoon of olive oil in a nonstick skillet over medium-high heat. Once the oil is shimmering, add the sausage and cook, using a wooden spoon to break it up into small pieces, until the sausage is browned and cooked through, about 5 minutes. Use a slotted spoon to transfer the sausage to a bowl and set aside.

Reduce the heat to medium and add the shallot, carrot, and mushrooms to the pan. Season with ½ teaspoon salt and ¼ teaspoon pepper and stir to combine. If the pan starts to look dry, add another splash of olive oil. Cook until the vegetables are beginning to soften, about 3 minutes. Add the apple and cranberries and stir to combine. Cook until the cranberries are glossy and beginning to rehydrate. Add the garlic and walnuts and cook until the garlic is fragrant, about 1 minute. Remove from the heat and transfer the mixture to the bowl with the sausage.

Add the cooked rice to the bowl with the sausage and vegetables and stir to combine. Season to taste with salt and pepper. Set the mixture aside to cool slightly.

Pat the hens dry inside and out. Tuck the wing tips under the body of the hens to prevent them from burning in the oven. Working with one hen at a time, season the inside of the cavity with salt and pepper. Hold the hen so the cavity is facing up. Spoon the filling into the cavity, using the back of the spoon to push the rice mixture down to fill the cavity. Use kitchen twine to tie the legs closed and place breast side up on the prepared baking sheet. Repeat with the remaining hens and filling.

Combine the mustard and 1 tablespoon of olive oil in a small bowl. Use a silicone brush to mix until evenly combined. Brush the mustard mixture onto the hens and season generously with salt and pepper. Roast for 60 minutes, until the skin is golden brown and crispy, the hens register 165°F on an instant-read thermometer, and the juices run clear. The stuffing should be 165°F.

Let rest for 10 minutes before serving.

Crispy Chicken Thighs with Radishes and Fennel

Oh this dish. It's simple, and it combines two of my favorite root vegetables with one of my favorite ways to prepare chicken. I jump at any chance to use fennel. Oddly, I don't like black licorice, but I love the hint of it in fennel. Make sure you get the chicken skin nice and crispy. As soon as I sit down, I pull it off and eat that first. It's my favorite part, and I'm sure you're going to love it, too.

For the Seasoning Blend

1 tablespoon dried parsley

1 tablespoon onion powder

1 tablespoon garlic powder

2 teaspoons freshly ground black pepper

1 tablespoon celery salt

For the Chicken

1½ pounds bone-in, skin-on chicken thighs (5 to 6 thighs)

2 tablespoons extra virgin olive oil

2 small fennel bulbs, trimmed, halved, and sliced (reserve fronds for garnish)

2 leeks, dark green parts discarded, light green and white part halved, sliced, and cleaned

2 bunches green onions, white and light green parts sliced into ½-inch pieces

2 bunches radishes, trimmed and halved

3 garlic cloves, grated

¼ cup dry white wine, such as pinot grigio or sauvignon blanc

Preheat the oven to 400°F.

To make the seasoning blend, blend the dried parsley in a spice grinder until it's fine. If you don't have a spice grinder, you can also do this by crushing the parsley leaves with your fingers. Transfer it to a small bowl and add the onion powder, garlic powder, pepper, and celery salt and stir until evenly combined.

To make the chicken, pat the chicken thighs dry and season the skin side with 2 teaspoons of the seasoning blend.

Heat a large oven-safe pan over medium heat. Once the pan is hot, add the olive oil. Transfer the chicken to the pan, skin side down. Cook, undisturbed, until the chicken skin is golden brown and releases easily from the pan, 5 to 8 minutes. Season the flesh side of the chicken with another 2 teaspoons of the seasoning blend. Flip and cook for an additional 4 minutes. Transfer the chicken to a plate and set aside. The chicken does not need to be fully cooked at this point; it will continue to cook in the oven.

Add the fennel, leeks, green onions, and radishes to the pan. Cook until the green onions are beginning to soften, about 3 minutes. Add the garlic and cook until just fragrant, about 1 minute. Next, add the wine to deglaze the pan, scraping up any browned bits from the bottom of the pan. Cook until the harsh alcohol smell burns off, then add the stock and mustard. Season with 1 teaspoon of the seasoning blend and stir to combine. Remove from the heat and add the chicken and any accumulated juices back to the pan, nestling the thighs into the vegetable mixture.

¼ cup low-sodium
   chicken stock

1 tablespoon Dijon mustard

Rice or mashed potatoes,
   for serving

Transfer the pan to the oven and roast for 25 to 35 minutes, until the chicken is golden brown and cooked through and the vegetables are soft.

Let the chicken rest for 5 minutes before serving. Garnish with fennel fronds and serve with rice or mashed potatoes.

Ginger Miso Chicken Wrap

For years, I ordered wraps similar to this in restaurants when I was traveling, and each time I bit into one and got that burst of tangy ginger miso dressing and grilled chicken, I thought to myself, *I should make this at home.* I did, and now you can, too. The mix of crunch and flavors in this wrap is a guaranteed crowd-pleaser.

½ head savoy cabbage, thinly shredded (about 3 cups)

1 large carrot, grated (about 1 cup)

5 radishes, cut into matchsticks

2 tablespoons chopped cilantro

⅓ cup Ginger Miso Dressing (page 326)

2 burrito-size tortillas

1 Meal Prep Grilled Chicken Breast (page 191), sliced

Toss the cabbage, carrot, radishes, and cilantro with the miso dressing in a large bowl.

Lay the tortillas on a clean work surface. Divide the slaw evenly between the tortillas, placing it in the center. Place the sliced chicken on top of the slaw. Roll the tortilla up like a burrito, encasing the slaw and chicken.

Heat a large nonstick skillet over medium-high heat. Place the wraps, seam side down, in the pan. Cook until the tortilla is crisp and lightly golden, 1 to 2 minutes. Flip and continue to cook until the other side is crisp, 1 more minute.

Transfer to a plate. Cut each wrap in half and serve.

Gumbo-Inspired Chicken Thighs and Rice

I love gumbo, but I don't always have the time or patience to spend all day making it. So I have instead spent time thinking of ways to approximate its flavor, and this dish gets right to the point while leaving your day free for things other than watching your pot simmer.

1½ pounds bone-in, skin-on chicken thighs (5 to 6 thighs)

Kosher salt and freshly ground black pepper

1 tablespoon extra virgin olive oil

8 ounces andouille sausage, cut on a bias into ¼-inch slices

2 tablespoons unsalted butter

1 yellow onion, diced

1 green bell pepper, diced

2 celery stalks, diced

½ to 1 teaspoon Cajun seasoning (depending on desired spice level)

1 teaspoon gumbo filé

½ teaspoon dried thyme

4 garlic cloves, chopped

2 cups frozen sliced okra

1 cup white rice

1½ cups low-sodium chicken stock

1 tablespoon apple cider vinegar

One 10-ounce can diced tomatoes and green chiles

Chopped parsley, for garnish

Pat the chicken thighs dry and season both sides generously with salt and pepper.

Heat the olive oil in a large high-sided pan over medium-high heat. Once the oil is shimmering, add the chicken thighs, skin side down, in an even layer. Cook, undisturbed, until the skin is golden brown and releases easily from the pan, 5 to 8 minutes. Flip and cook for an additional 4 minutes. Transfer the chicken to a plate and set aside. The chicken does not need to be fully cooked at this point; it will continue to cook with the rice later.

Reduce the heat to medium, add the andouille, and cook, stirring occasionally, until the sausage is browned, about 3 minutes. Use a slotted spoon to transfer the sausage to the plate with the chicken.

Add the butter to the hot pan. Once it melts, add the onion, bell pepper, and celery and stir to combine. Season with the Cajun seasoning, gumbo filé, thyme, ½ teaspoon salt, and ¼ teaspoon pepper and cook, stirring occasionally, until the vegetables have softened, about 5 minutes. Add the garlic and okra and cook until the okra no longer looks frozen and icy, about 3 minutes.

Add the rice to the pan and stir to combine with the vegetables. Season with ½ teaspoon salt and ¼ teaspoon pepper. Increase the heat to high and add the stock, vinegar, and diced tomatoes and green chiles. Bring the mixture to a boil and add the chicken and the sausage back to the pan, nestling the chicken into the stock and rice. Reduce the heat to low, cover, and cook until the liquid has been absorbed by the rice and the chicken is cooked through, 15 minutes.

Remove from the heat and let sit, covered, for 5 minutes. Serve garnished with parsley.

Honey Ginger Chicken Wings

Whether it's dinner for one, two, or more, it's a party as soon as you set a bowl of freshly cooked crispy chicken wings on the table. And when they're slathered with gingered honey, I mean, come on. I don't have to say anything more because I know you can already taste them.

Cooking spray

1½ pounds chicken wings, a mixture of flats and drumettes

1½ teaspoons baking powder

1½ teaspoons kosher salt

½ teaspoon freshly ground black pepper

2 tablespoons unsalted butter

1 tablespoon Turmeric Ginger Honey (page 311)

1 tablespoon low-sodium soy sauce

2 garlic cloves, grated

1 teaspoon grated ginger

Toasted sesame seeds, for garnish

Sliced green onions, for garnish

Preheat the oven to 425°F. Line a baking sheet with foil and set a wire rack inside. Spray the rack lightly with cooking spray.

Pat the chicken wings dry and place them in a large bowl. Sprinkle the baking powder, salt, and pepper over the wings and toss to coat. Transfer the wings to the prepared rack, leaving a little room between each piece. Bake for 45 to 50 minutes, flipping at the 20-minute mark and at the 40-minute mark. The wings should be golden and crisp on both sides.

Meanwhile, melt the butter in a small saucepan over medium-low heat. Add the honey, soy sauce, garlic, and ginger and stir to combine. Cook until the garlic is fragrant but not browned, about 1 minute. Remove from the heat and cover to keep warm until the wings are ready.

Transfer the wings to a bowl. Add the sauce and toss to coat.

Transfer the wings to a serving platter and garnish with sesame seeds and sliced green onions.

Jalapeño Popper Chicken Breasts

Someone asked, "How did you come up with this recipe?" I hate answering a question with a question, but how did people come up with a bacon cheeseburger? A chocolate-dipped peanut butter pretzel? Franks and beans? I simply took everything I loved in a jalapeño popper, stuffed it under the skin of a chicken breast, and have enjoyed it ever since.

6 ounces cream cheese, room temperature

¼ cup finely chopped shallot (from 1 large shallot)

⅓ cup finely chopped jalapeño (from 1 large or 2 small jalapeños)

2 garlic cloves, grated

Kosher salt and freshly ground black pepper

4 bone-in, skin-on chicken breasts

2 tablespoons extra virgin olive oil

Preheat the oven to 400°F. Line a baking sheet with parchment paper.

Combine the cream cheese, shallot, jalapeño, garlic, and ½ teaspoon salt in a small bowl. Use a silicone spatula to mix until evenly combined.

Pat the chicken dry and place on the prepared baking sheet. Create a small pocket between the skin and the meat by gently sliding your fingers under the skin and separating the skin from the meat, leaving the edges intact. Be careful not to completely separate the skin from the chicken breast; this pocket will hold the cream cheese mixture and ensure that it won't all melt out. Use your hands to transfer the cream cheese mixture under the skin of each of the chicken breasts and smooth the mixture out from the top of the skin to create an even layer.

Drizzle the chicken with the olive oil and season generously with salt and pepper. Roast for 30 to 35 minutes, until the skin is crisp and the chicken registers 165°F on an instant-read thermometer. Let rest for 5 minutes before serving.

Kumquat Ginger Braised Chicken Thighs

The kumquat tree in my backyard produces a ton of fruit. A few years ago, I used the bounty of 'quats to make kumquat-cello. Since then, I have come up with other ways to use them, this dish being one I come back to again and again for the thrill of all these flavors.

1 cup kumquats

1½ pounds bone-in chicken thighs (5 to 6 thighs)

Kosher salt and freshly ground black pepper

Extra virgin olive oil

2 red onions, halved and sliced

¼ cup chopped cilantro stems, plus chopped cilantro, for garnish

2 teaspoons grated ginger

4 garlic cloves, grated

1 teaspoon lemon zest

1 tablespoon Turmeric Ginger Honey (page 311)

1 cup low-sodium chicken stock

2 tablespoons freshly squeezed lemon juice

Cooked rice, for serving

Lemon wedges, for garnish

Slice the kumquats into rounds. To remove the seeds, gently squeeze any rounds with seeds; they should pop right out. Set aside.

Pat the chicken thighs dry and season both sides generously with salt and pepper.

Heat 2 tablespoons of olive oil in a large pan or Dutch oven over medium heat. Once the oil is shimmering, add the chicken, skin side down. Cook, undisturbed, until the chicken is golden brown and releases easily from the pan, 5 to 8 minutes. Flip and cook for an additional 4 minutes. Transfer the chicken to a plate and set aside. The chicken does not need to be fully cooked at this point; it will continue to cook later.

Add the onions to the pan and season with a pinch of salt and pepper. Add ¼ cup of water to the pan to deglaze it, scraping up any browned bits from the bottom of the pan. Cook the onions, stirring occasionally, until they have reduced in volume by half and are very soft and translucent, about 10 minutes. If the pan starts to look too dry, add in another splash of olive oil or lower the heat slightly.

Once the onions have cooked down, add the cilantro stems, sliced kumquats, ginger, garlic, lemon zest, and honey to the pan. Stir to combine and cook until the garlic and ginger are fragrant, about 1 minute. Add the stock and lemon juice to deglaze, scraping up any remaining browned bits from the bottom of the pan. Bring the mixture to a boil, then reduce the heat to low. Return the chicken and any accumulated juices to the pan, nestling it into the stock mixture. Cover the pan and cook until the chicken shreds easily with a fork, 35 to 45 minutes.

Serve the chicken and sauce over rice. Garnish with cilantro and lemon wedges.

Lemon Pepper Chicken Wings

PHOTO ON PAGE 185

I received a lot of positive reactions after I made a version of this on *Valerie's Home Cooking*, but some requested a variation for people who don't like a ton of spice on their wings, so I came up with this recipe. However, if you're like me and tend to add a tad more zest, juice, and other spices than called for, feel free to season to your own taste.

Cooking spray

1½ pounds chicken wings, a mixture of flats and drumettes

1½ teaspoons baking powder

1½ teaspoons kosher salt

1 teaspoon freshly ground black pepper, plus more for garnish (optional)

2 tablespoons unsalted butter

1 teaspoon lemon zest

1 tablespoon freshly squeezed lemon juice

2 garlic cloves, grated

Chopped parsley, for garnish

Preheat the oven to 425°F. Line a baking sheet with foil and set a wire rack inside. Spray the rack lightly with cooking spray.

Pat the chicken wings dry and place them in a large bowl. Sprinkle the baking powder, salt, and ½ teaspoon of the pepper over the wings and toss to coat them. Transfer the wings to the prepared rack, leaving a little room between each piece. Bake for 45 to 50 minutes, flipping at the 20-minute mark and at the 40-minute mark. The wings should be golden and crisp on both sides.

Meanwhile, about 10 minutes before the wings are done, melt the butter in a small saucepan over medium-low heat. Add the lemon zest, lemon juice, garlic, and remaining ½ teaspoon pepper and stir to combine. Cook until the garlic is fragrant but not browned, about 1 minute. Remove from the heat and cover to keep warm until the wings are ready.

Transfer the wings to a bowl. Add the sauce and toss to coat.

Transfer the wings to a serving platter and garnish with parsley and more black pepper, if using.

Meal Prep Grilled Chicken Breasts

PHOTO ON PAGE 170

I'm into meal preparation, and I find it convenient to have some cooked chicken breasts ready in my fridge. Basic stuff, but it saves time and comes in handy. I usually sauté them on the stove, but during grilling season, I buy a value pack and cook them up. This way, I can easily use them in various meals for the next few days.

1 teaspoon kosher salt

¼ teaspoon freshly ground pepper

¼ teaspoon ground cumin

½ teaspoon smoked paprika

½ teaspoon onion powder

½ teaspoon garlic powder

½ teaspoon chili powder

4 boneless, skinless chicken breasts

1 tablespoon extra virgin olive oil

Preheat the grill to 400°F and prepare part of the grill for indirect grilling.

Combine the salt, pepper, cumin, smoked paprika, onion powder, garlic powder, and chili powder in a large bowl. Mix to evenly combine. Add the chicken to the bowl with the seasoning, drizzle with the olive oil, and toss the chicken in the seasoning to coat.

Transfer the chicken to the grill and cook, undisturbed, for 3 minutes, until nice grill marks have formed. Flip the chicken and cook for an additional 3 minutes. Move the chicken to the indirect side of the grill, close the cover of the grill, and cook until the chicken reaches 160°F on an instant-read thermometer, an additional 3 to 5 minutes. Transfer the chicken to a plate and let rest for 5 minutes. The chicken will continue cooking after it's removed from the grill and will come up to 165°F.

Serve immediately or let cool completely and store in an airtight container in the fridge for up to 4 days.

Mediterranean Chicken Thighs with Potatoes, Peppers, and Feta

When I make this dish, I can close my eyes and easily imagine having dinner on the balcony of some chic restaurant overlooking the Mediterranean Sea. While the recipe calls for many ingredients, the process of chopping up all the fresh vegetables and potatoes, and then breathing in the aromatic flavors of the herbs and seasonings as they infuse the chicken, sets the mood for a delightful meal.

6 bone-in, skin-on
  chicken thighs

Kosher salt and freshly
  ground black pepper

2 tablespoons extra virgin
  olive oil

1 yellow onion, halved
  and sliced

1 red bell pepper, sliced
  into strips

1 yellow bell pepper, sliced
  into strips

¾ teaspoon red pepper flakes

8 ounces baby Yukon Gold
  potatoes, quartered

3 garlic cloves, thinly sliced

1 cup cherry tomatoes

½ cup red wine vinegar

1 tablespoon
  chopped oregano

1 tablespoon thyme leaves

One 12-ounce jar quartered
  artichoke hearts, drained

⅓ cup crumbled feta

2 tablespoons chopped
  parsley, for garnish

Preheat the oven to 400°F.

Pat the chicken thighs dry and season the skin side with salt and pepper.

Heat the olive oil in a large, high-sided, oven-safe pan over medium-high heat. Once the oil is shimmering, add the chicken, skin side down. Season the flesh side of the chicken with salt and pepper. Cook, undisturbed, until the chicken is golden brown and releases easily from the pan, 5 to 8 minutes. Flip and cook for an additional 2 minutes. Transfer the chicken to a plate and set aside. The chicken does not need to be fully cooked at this point; it will continue to cook in the oven.

Reduce the heat to medium and add the onion, bell peppers, and pepper flakes to the pan. Sprinkle with salt. Cook, stirring regularly, until the vegetables are slightly wilted, about 3 minutes. The liquid from the vegetables will help deglaze the pan. Add the potatoes and garlic, sprinkle with salt, and cook, stirring occasionally, for an additional 3 minutes. Add the tomatoes, vinegar, oregano, thyme, and artichoke hearts. Sprinkle with salt and pepper and stir to combine. Remove from the heat and add the chicken and accumulated juices back to the pan, nestling the thighs into the vegetables.

Transfer the pan to the oven and bake, uncovered, for about 35 minutes, until the internal temperature of the chicken reaches 165°F on an instant-read thermometer and the potatoes are fork-tender. Sprinkle with the feta and parsley and serve.

Mom's Roasted Chicken and Vegetables

This recipe was one of my mother's go-to dishes, and I believe anyone who wants to be comfortable in the kitchen should not only know how to make a good roast chicken and vegetables but also have it in regular monthly rotation for one very good reason—it's absolutely delicious. A chicken roasted on a bed of vegetables, with all those flowing, succulent juices—and done in one pan—might also be the perfect dinner.

5 medium carrots, cut into large chunks

1 pound baby Yukon Gold potatoes, halved

1 bulb garlic, broken into cloves but not peeled

1 yellow onion, halved through the root

Extra virgin olive oil

Kosher salt and freshly ground black pepper

⅓ cup dry white wine

One 3- to 4-pound chicken

½ lemon, quartered

4 thyme sprigs

4 rosemary sprigs

½ teaspoon onion powder

½ teaspoon garlic powder

½ teaspoon Italian seasoning

Go-To Gravy (page 335; optional)

Preheat the oven to 400°F.

Place the carrots, potatoes, and garlic cloves in a 9 × 13-inch baking dish. Cut half of the onion into ½-inch strips and add that to the baking dish with the veggies. Cut the other half into large chunks and set aside. Drizzle the vegetables with 2 tablespoons of olive oil, season generously with salt and pepper, and toss to combine. Pour the wine over the vegetables and set aside.

Remove the giblets from the chicken and discard. Pat the chicken dry and remove any excess fat from the opening of the chicken. Season the inside liberally with salt and pepper. Stuff the cavity with the lemon, onion chunks, thyme, and rosemary. Tie the legs together with kitchen twine and tuck the wing tips under the body of the chicken.

Drizzle the chicken with 2 tablespoons of olive oil and season generously with salt and pepper. Sprinkle the chicken with the onion powder, garlic powder, and Italian seasoning. Place the chicken on top of the vegetables and transfer to the oven. Roast for 1 hour 20 minutes to 1 hour 30 minutes, until the chicken skin is crisp and the breast reaches an internal temperature of 155°F on an instant-read thermometer; the chicken will continue to cook as it rests and will come up to 165°F.

Tent the chicken with foil and let rest for 10 minutes before carving. Serve with the roasted vegetables and gravy (if using).

One-Pan Honey Mustard Chicken Thighs

If you're having one of those days when you're juggling a lot but still want to prepare a lovely meal, keep this dish in mind. The prep is quick and simple. After you crisp up the chicken, you add vegetables, slide the pan into the oven for less than an hour—and voilà! This dish not only plates beautifully family-style, it tastes even better than it looks.

6 bone-in, skin-on
  chicken thighs

Kosher salt and freshly
  ground black pepper

2 tablespoons vegetable oil

½ cup dry white wine, such as
  pinot grigio

One 14-ounce bag frozen
  pearl onions

4 garlic cloves, thinly sliced

¼ cup low-sodium
  chicken stock

3 tablespoons honey mustard

8 ounces cremini mushrooms,
  quartered

1 tablespoon fresh
  thyme leaves

1 cup frozen petite peas

Preheat the oven to 400°F.

Pat the chicken thighs dry and sprinkle the skin side generously with salt and pepper.

Heat 1 tablespoon of the vegetable oil in a large, high-sided, oven-safe pan over medium-high heat. Once the oil is shimmering, add the chicken thighs, skin side down. (Depending on the size of your chicken thighs, you may need to work in batches to avoid crowding the pan.) Sprinkle the flesh side of the chicken generously with salt and pepper. Cook until the skin is golden brown, crispy, and releases easily from the pan, 5 to 8 minutes. Flip and cook for an additional 2 minutes. Transfer the chicken to a plate and set aside. The chicken does not need to be fully cooked at this point; it will continue to cook in the oven.

Reduce the heat to medium-low and pour in the wine. Cook, scraping up any browned bits from the bottom of the pan, until the harsh alcohol smell burns off and the wine has slightly reduced, about 1 minute. Add the frozen onions and garlic and cook until fragrant, about 2 minutes. Add the stock and 2 tablespoons of the honey mustard. Stir until the mixture is well combined and emulsified. Add the mushrooms and thyme to the pan and stir to coat the mushrooms in the mixture.

Remove from the heat and add the chicken and any accumulated juices back to the pan, nestling the thighs into the vegetable mixture. Whisk together the remaining 1 tablespoon honey mustard and 1 tablespoon oil in a small bowl. Use a silicone brush to brush the tops of the chicken thighs with the honey mustard mixture.

Transfer the chicken to the oven and bake for 35 to 40 minutes, until the vegetables are browned and the chicken registers 165°F on an instant-read thermometer.

Turn the oven off. Remove the chicken from the oven and add the frozen peas. Stir slightly to submerge them in the sauce. Return the pan to the oven for another 2 to 3 minutes, until the peas are heated through.

To serve, plate the chicken and vegetables and top with the pan sauce.

Peanut Chicken with Collard Greens

I love the peanuts in kung pao chicken at Chinese restaurants. I also love putting peanuts on my ice cream and eating them plain at the ballpark. Okay, I love peanuts, period—which is the point of this hearty dish. Influences range from Mrs. Van Halen, who introduced me to peanut sauce way back when Ed and I were dating, to my fondness for collard greens that have simmered awhile on a loving stovetop. I think you'll love this one.

2 tablespoons avocado oil

4 bone-in, skin-on chicken breasts

Kosher salt and freshly ground black pepper

½ small yellow onion, finely diced (about ½ cup)

1 jalapeño, ribs and seeds removed, finely chopped

4 garlic cloves, grated

1½ tablespoons grated ginger

One 13.5-ounce can full-fat coconut milk

½ cup creamy peanut butter

2 tablespoons red curry paste

½ cup low-sodium chicken stock

1 bunch collard greens, ribs and stems removed and thinly sliced

6 tablespoons freshly squeezed lime juice (from 3 limes)

2 tablespoons low-sodium soy sauce

1 teaspoon fish sauce

Cooked white rice, for serving

Thai basil leaves, for garnish

Chopped cilantro, for garnish

Preheat the oven to 375°F. Line a baking sheet with parchment paper.

Heat the avocado oil in a large high-sided pan over medium heat. Pat the chicken breasts dry and season generously with salt and pepper. Once the oil is shimmering, add the chicken breasts, skin side down. Cook, undisturbed, until the skin is golden brown and crisp, about 5 minutes. Flip and cook for an additional 4 minutes. Transfer to the prepared baking sheet and reserve the pan for the collard greens. Roast the chicken for 20 to 30 minutes, until the internal temperature reaches 160°F on an instant-read thermometer. The exact time will depend on the size of the chicken breasts. Remove from the oven and let rest. The chicken will continue to cook as it rests and will come up to 165°F.

While the chicken is in the oven, add the onion and jalapeño to the reserved pan. Cook over low heat until the vegetables have softened, about 4 minutes. Add the garlic and ginger and cook until just fragrant, 20 to 30 seconds. Add the coconut milk, peanut butter, curry paste, and stock. Whisk the mixture until it comes together. Add the collard greens and cook, stirring occasionally, until they are tender but still have a little bite, about 15 minutes. Remove from the heat and add the lime juice, soy sauce, and fish sauce.

Cover and keep warm until the chicken is cooked and rested. Carefully remove the meat from the bone using a sharp knife. Slice the chicken breast against the grain in ½-inch slices.

To serve, spoon rice into bowls. Top with some of the sauce. Shingle the chicken on top and top with more sauce if desired, or serve extra sauce on the side. Garnish with Thai basil and cilantro.

MEAT

"I love when family and
friends walk in the door
and say, 'It smells delicious.
What's cooking?'"

Beef and Broccoli

I've been making this since my son was little and I finally got him to eat broccoli. Mrs. Van Halen tipped me off to the Asian influences. The dish is still in regular rotation in my kitchen because it's always satisfying, quick, and simple to make. Instead of serving it with rice, try a side of homemade potato chips or sweet potato fries, or enjoy it on its own as I usually do. The leftovers are great, too.

2 tablespoons cornstarch

1 teaspoon sesame oil

1 pound flank steak, sliced against the grain into 1-inch pieces

½ cup low-sodium soy sauce

2 teaspoons rice vinegar

1 tablespoon light brown sugar

½ teaspoon red pepper flakes

4 garlic cloves, grated

2 teaspoons grated ginger

1 tablespoon neutral oil, such as avocado oil or grapeseed oil

4 cups small broccoli florets

Cooked white rice, for serving

1 tablespoon toasted sesame seeds, for garnish

Whisk together 1 tablespoon of the cornstarch with 2 tablespoons of water in a large bowl until smooth. Add the sesame oil and whisk to combine. Add the sliced steak and toss to coat the steak in the mixture. Set aside while you make the sauce.

In a small bowl, whisk together the remaining 1 tablespoon cornstarch, the soy sauce, rice vinegar, brown sugar, pepper flakes, garlic, and ginger. Set aside.

Heat the neutral oil in a large nonstick skillet over medium-high heat. Once the oil is shimmering, add the beef and cook, stirring occasionally, until almost cooked through and browned in places, about 5 minutes. Using a slotted spoon, transfer the beef to a plate. Set aside.

Reduce the heat to medium and add the broccoli to the hot pan with 2 tablespoons of water. Cook until tender, 3 to 5 minutes.

Return the beef and any remaining juices from the plate to the pan with the broccoli. Add the sauce and stir until evenly combined.

Serve the beef and broccoli over rice and garnish with sesame seeds.

Classic Double Cheeseburger with Special Sauce

When I'm traveling solo, I still like to sit at the hotel bar with a big, juicy cheeseburger, a glass of red wine, and a good novel. The meal hits all the right notes. I know the urge is to serve this with a side of fries, but you can also pair with a small, simple salad or indulge as is and let your biggest decision be whether to pick it up with your hands or use a knife and fork.

For the Special Sauce

¼ cup mayonnaise

3 tablespoons ketchup

1 tablespoon yellow mustard

1 tablespoon dill relish

1 teaspoon
   Worcestershire sauce

For the Double Cheeseburgers

2 pounds ground beef
   (80% lean)

Kosher salt and freshly
   ground black pepper

12 slices American cheese

6 hamburger buns (page
   122 or store-bought),
   split and lightly toasted

1 large tomato, sliced

½ red onion, thinly sliced
   into rings

1½ cups shredded
   iceberg lettuce

To make the sauce, stir together the mayo, ketchup, mustard, relish, and Worcestershire sauce in a medium bowl. Set aside.

To make the cheeseburgers, prepare a grill for cooking over medium-high heat.

Divide the ground beef into twelve equal portions. Roll each portion into a ball, then flatten it into a thin 4-inch patty. Lightly sprinkle one side of the patties with salt and pepper. Grill, seasoned side down, until about halfway cooked, about 3 minutes. Before flipping the patties, sprinkle the other side with salt and pepper, top each with a slice of cheese, and continue to cook until the patties are cooked through and the cheese has begun to melt, 1 to 2 minutes more.

Build each burger on a bun with two patties, tomato, onion, lettuce, and a generous slathering of special sauce.

Filet Mignon with Béarnaise Sauce

There is something elegant about sitting down to a beautifully cut filet mignon with a splash of béarnaise sauce. In fact, just saying "béarnaise" makes me feel more sophisticated. Kidding aside, this was one of Ed's favorite meals when we went out for a special occasion. Then I started making it at home, turning any old night into a special occasion evening, which is the point of this cookbook.

For the Béarnaise Sauce

- 2 tablespoons white wine vinegar
- 2 tablespoons dry white wine, such as sauvignon blanc
- 1 shallot, finely minced
- 1 tablespoon finely chopped tarragon leaves
- Kosher salt and freshly ground black pepper
- 3 large egg yolks, room temperature
- ¾ cup ghee, melted

For the Filet Mignon

- 2 tablespoons extra virgin olive oil
- Four 6-ounce filets mignons (at room temperature for 30 minutes)
- Kosher salt and freshly ground black pepper
- ½ stick (4 tablespoons) unsalted butter
- 4 garlic cloves
- 2 rosemary sprigs

Preheat the oven to 400°F.

Meanwhile, to make the béarnaise sauce, combine the vinegar, wine, shallot, tarragon, and ¼ teaspoon pepper in a small saucepan. Bring to a boil over medium heat, then reduce the heat to low and simmer until slightly reduced, 2 minutes. Transfer to a metal bowl to cool.

Add the egg yolks and 1 tablespoon of water to the bowl with the cooled vinegar mixture. Whisk to combine.

Set up a double boiler: Fill a medium pot with an inch or so of hot water. Be sure that the base of the bowl with the vinegar mixture doesn't touch the water in the saucepan. Turn the heat to low and place the bowl on the pot. Whisk continuously until the eggs have doubled in size and thickened, about 5 minutes. Slowly stream in the melted ghee 2 tablespoons at a time while whisking. Be sure that the ghee is fully emulsified in the egg mixture before adding more. Once all the ghee has been added, add water 1 tablespoon at a time to thin the sauce to your desired consistency. Season to taste with salt and pepper. Set aside until ready to use. Reheat the sauce over a double boiler if needed before serving.

To make the filets, heat the olive oil in a cast-iron skillet over medium-high heat. Season the filets generously with salt and pepper. Once the oil is hot, add the steaks and cook, undisturbed, until nicely seared, 4 minutes. Flip and add the butter, garlic, and rosemary. Cook for another 4 minutes, occasionally basting the meat with the butter, garlic, and rosemary. Transfer the pan to the oven and cook for 5 minutes. Check the temperature of the meat: 135°F for medium-rare. Let the filets rest for 10 minutes before serving with the sauce.

Have
Leftovers?

Turn it into a delicious sandwich by tossing arugula in lightly heated béarnaise sauce and layering it on top of sliced steak on a ciabatta roll.

Italian Meatloaf

Years ago, I adapted my mom's and grandmother's recipe for meatballs into a delicious and decadent Italian meatloaf for a very specific reason: I wanted to make a meatball sandwich, but one in which the meatballs wouldn't fall out. I took a slice from the meatloaf, and it was perfect on some great crusty bread with mayo and arugula.

1 tablespoon extra virgin olive oil

1 yellow onion, finely chopped

1 teaspoon Italian seasoning

1¼ teaspoons kosher salt

½ teaspoon freshly ground black pepper

1 tablespoon unsalted butter

3 garlic cloves, grated

1 large egg

1 pound ground beef

1 pound spicy Italian sausage

⅓ cup Italian-style bread crumbs

⅓ cup freshly grated Parmesan (about 1½ ounces)

½ cup packed basil leaves

6 slices provolone

¼ cup ketchup

½ teaspoon Calabrian chili paste

Heat the olive oil in a nonstick skillet over medium heat. Once the oil is shimmering, add the onion, Italian seasoning, ½ teaspoon of the salt, and ¼ teaspoon of the pepper. Cook, stirring occasionally, until the onion is soft and translucent, about 5 minutes. Add the butter to the pan. Once it's melted, add the garlic and cook until well combined and fragrant, 1 to 2 minutes. Remove from the heat and transfer the mixture to a bowl to cool to room temperature.

Preheat the oven to 375°F. Line a baking sheet with parchment paper.

Once the onion mixture is cooled, crack the egg into the bowl and whisk to break up the yolk. Add the remaining ¾ teaspoon salt and ¼ teaspoon pepper and stir to combine. Add the ground beef and sausage, breaking it up into small pieces as you add it to the bowl. Sprinkle the bread crumbs and Parmesan over the meat. Use clean hands or a spatula to mix everything together until evenly combined.

Place a large piece of wax paper on a clean work surface. Transfer the meat mixture to the wax paper and flatten it out into a 10 × 13-inch rectangle. Evenly distribute the basil over the meat, leaving a 1-inch border all the way around. Top with the sliced provolone. Starting on one long end, roll up the meat like a jelly roll, using the wax paper to help you roll, peeling it back as you go. Seal the seam of the meatloaf and the ends, totally encasing the cheese. Use your hands to smooth and compact the meat into a tight roll. You should end up with a meatloaf that is 11 to 12 inches long. Transfer the meatloaf to the prepared baking sheet.

Mix together the ketchup and chili paste in a small bowl. Spoon the mixture over the top of the meatloaf. Bake for 45 to 50 minutes, until the meatloaf registers 160°F on an instant-read thermometer.

Let rest for 10 minutes before slicing and serving.

Ketjap Sambal Marinated Rib Eye

The rib eye is my favorite cut of meat. It's tender and full of flavor. In a restaurant, I order it medium-rare so I can eat around the edges where it's more medium and then reheat the rare leftovers the next day. This rib eye is comfort food pure and simple, and marinating it in ketjap sambal, a sweet and very spicy mix of two sauces that Mrs. Van Halen taught me to make forever ago, gives every bite of this steak a pleasing zing. I say indulge!

1 tablespoon canola oil

2 teaspoons minced garlic

2 teaspoons grated ginger

2 teaspoons minced seeded jalapeño (optional)

¼ cup packed light brown sugar

¼ cup tamari

½ teaspoon five-spice powder

½ to 1 teaspoon Sambal Oelek (page 328 or store-bought)

2 bone-in rib eye steaks, 1 inch thick (about 1¼ pounds)

Kosher salt and freshly ground black pepper

2 tablespoons extra virgin olive oil

To make the marinade, heat the canola oil in a small saucepan over medium-high heat. Add the garlic, ginger, and jalapeño (if using). Sauté until fragrant but not browned, 2 to 3 minutes. Add the brown sugar, tamari, five-spice powder, and ½ cup of water. Bring the mixture to a simmer and cook until the sauce reduces and coats the back of a spoon, about 10 minutes. Transfer the sauce to a bowl and stir in the sambal. Let cool to room temperature.

Add the steaks and the cooled marinade to a zip-top bag. Move the steaks around to coat them in the marinade. Let marinate for 30 minutes at room temperature or up to 6 hours in the fridge. If marinating in the fridge, remove the steaks 30 minutes before cooking.

Line a baking sheet with paper towels. Remove the steaks from the marinade and place them on the paper towels to blot off any excess marinade. Season with salt and pepper.

Heat the olive oil in a cast-iron skillet over medium-high heat. When the oil is just smoking, add the steaks to the pan and cook, undisturbed, for 4 minutes. Flip and cook for an additional 4 minutes. Transfer to a plate and let rest for 10 minutes. Slice off the bone and serve.

Have Leftovers?

Slather mayo on an Italian sub roll, top with sliced steak, Quick-Pickled Vegetables (page 57), and cilantro.

Pork Chops with Cabbage and Apple

Pork chops sizzling on the stovetop before being transferred to the oven takes me straight back to my childhood home, where I can see my mom making dinner. If my brothers or I were distracting her, which was often the case, she was guaranteed at some point to exclaim, "Shoot, I overcooked the pork chops." So to ensure maximum juiciness, you should take the temperature of these chops as they cook. The cabbage and apples make each bite an exquisite chew.

2 bone-in, center-cut pork loin chops, 1 to 1½ inches thick (1½ pounds)

Kosher salt and freshly ground black pepper

2 tablespoons extra virgin olive oil

½ large head green cabbage, roughly chopped (about 7 cups)

1 Honeycrisp apple, chopped

1 teaspoon fish sauce

½ cup low-sodium chicken stock

2 garlic cloves, minced

1 tablespoon chives, for garnish

Preheat the oven to 400°F.

Season the pork chops generously with salt and pepper. Heat the olive oil in a large high-sided, oven-safe pan over medium heat. Once the oil is shimmering, add the pork chops. Cook until a nice golden crust has formed, 4 to 5 minutes. Flip and cook for an additional 3 minutes. Transfer the pork chops to a plate and set aside. The pork chops do not have to be fully cooked at this point; they will continue to cook in the oven.

Add the cabbage, apple, and fish sauce to the pan and stir to combine. Pour in the stock to deglaze the pan, scraping up any browned bits from the bottom of the pan. Add the garlic, ¾ teaspoon salt, and ¼ teaspoon pepper and cook until the garlic is fragrant, 30 seconds to 1 minute. Season to taste with salt and pepper. Remove from the heat and return the pork chops and any accumulated juices to the pan, nestling them into the cabbage mixture.

Transfer the pan to the oven and bake for 10 to 15 minutes, until the pork registers 155°F on an instant-read thermometer. Let rest for 10 minutes before slicing. The pork will continue to cook as it rests.

To serve, remove the meat from the bone and slice. Serve with the cabbage mixture and any pan sauce. Garnish with extra black pepper and chives.

Prime Rib with Horseradish Sauce

A true classic, this prime rib is for when you want to celebrate or spoil that special someone in your life. It's about as indulgent as it gets. The dish is all about the prep. To bring out the best flavor, let the prime rib sit in the fridge for a few days to dry out, as they do in the finest restaurants. If possible, make the horseradish sauce in the morning so the flavor intensifies by dinnertime. Serve with Classic Mashed Potatoes (page 220) and Chive Popovers (page 124) on the side.

1 first-cut 3-bone prime rib roast (about 6½ pounds; also called standing rib roast)

⅓ cup freshly grated peeled horseradish (from about a 5-ounce piece)

1¼ cups crème fraîche or sour cream

2 teaspoons white wine vinegar

½ teaspoon sugar

Kosher salt and freshly ground black pepper

2 bunches rosemary

2 bunches sage

2 bunches thyme

1 tablespoon extra virgin olive oil

Flaky sea salt, for serving

Pat the prime rib dry. Refrigerate, uncovered, for at least 1 day and up to 3 days to age the meat.

To make the horseradish sauce, at least 4 hours and up to 1 day before serving, mix together the horseradish, crème fraîche, vinegar, and sugar in a medium bowl and season to taste with salt and pepper. Refrigerate until ready to serve.

Preheat the oven to 225°F. Toss the rosemary, sage, and thyme with the olive oil and arrange on the bottom of a roasting pan. Season the prime rib generously with salt and pepper, then set it on top of the herbs.

Roast until an instant-read thermometer inserted into the center of the prime rib registers 125°F, 3 hours 15 minutes to 4 hours. Remove from the oven and let rest at least 30 minutes and up to 1 hour. As the prime rib rests, the residual heat will bring the internal temp up another 5 degrees, giving you a medium-rare roast.

Increase the oven temperature to 500°F. Right before serving, return the rested prime rib to the oven and roast until the outside is browned and caramelized, about 10 minutes.

Transfer the prime rib to a cutting board. Using a sharp chef's knife, cut the meat away from the bones, then slice the meat across the grain.

Serve with the crispy herbs, horseradish sauce, and flaky salt.

Have Leftovers?

Turn them into roast beef sandwiches! Mix leftover horseradish sauce with mayo and slather on Italian bread. Top with slices of roast beef and arugula.

Slow-Cooker Pulled Pork with Shallots and Chiles

Whether you're cooking for a raucous football party, a family get-together, or just yourself, this dish is a winner. After six hours, the pork is irresistibly tender and flavorful. It's a good example of why I am in love with my slow cooker. In fact, outside of family and a few friends, the slow cooker is one of my longest and most fulfilling relationships. Serve the pork on its own or as amazing sandwiches or sliders.

For the Pulled Pork

3 pounds boneless pork shoulder, cut into 2-inch pieces

1 cup barbecue sauce

3 tablespoons light brown sugar

2 teaspoons chili powder

1 teaspoon chipotle powder

6 ounces light lager (optional)

3 tablespoons apple cider vinegar, plus a splash

Kosher salt

1 medium onion, thinly sliced

3 green onions, chopped

For the Fried Shallots and Chiles

Vegetable oil, for frying

2 egg whites

1½ cups all-purpose flour

1 teaspoon chili powder

1 teaspoon ground cumin

Kosher salt and freshly ground black pepper

4 Fresno chiles, sliced crosswise into rings

4 large shallots, sliced crosswise into rings

Celery salt, for seasoning

For the Sandwiches (optional)

12 slices white sandwich bread or 6 hamburger buns

Bread-and-butter pickles, for serving

To make the pulled pork, combine the pork, barbecue sauce, brown sugar, chili powder, chipotle powder, lager (if using), 3 tablespoons vinegar, 2 teaspoons salt, and the onion in a 6-quart slow cooker. Cook on high power for 6 hours.

With a slotted spoon, transfer the pork to a cutting board and shred using two forks. Transfer to a bowl and add enough of the liquid from the slow cooker to generously moisten it. Stir in the green onions and the splash of vinegar and season with salt to taste.

To make the fried shallots and chiles, set a wire rack in a baking sheet. Add enough oil to a medium saucepan to fill by 2 inches. Heat the oil to 340°F over medium heat. Meanwhile, in a medium bowl, whisk the egg whites with a fork until frothy. In a separate medium bowl, whisk together the flour, chili powder, cumin, and some salt and pepper. Working in batches, add the chiles and shallots to the bowl of egg whites and toss to coat. Allow any excess liquid to drain off, then coat in the flour mixture. Put the coated chiles and shallots onto the prepared wire rack. Fry in batches until golden brown, about 2 minutes. Transfer to a paper towel–lined baking sheet to drain and sprinkle with celery salt.

Serve the pulled pork topped with fried shallots and chiles, or to assemble into sandwiches, if desired, add the pulled pork to 6 slices of bread, then top with fried chiles and shallots, pickles, and the remaining 6 slices bread.

POTATOES

"I have yet to meet anyone
who doesn't love a good spud."

Turkey
Cottage Pie
(page 229)

Classic Mashed Potatoes

When in doubt, mash the potatoes! Especially if you're having people over. This classic is a guaranteed crowd-pleaser and a holiday staple. I didn't make them one Thanksgiving and everyone in the family flipped out. How could I? Well, I never skipped them again and never will. This recipe is very accepting of your tastes and traditions, whether you add sour cream, cheese, bacon, horseradish, or all of the above. But start with the basic. It will serve you well. I can vouch for it.

2 pounds russet potatoes, peeled and cut into 2-inch chunks

4 garlic cloves, smashed

Kosher salt and freshly ground black pepper

1 cup milk

6 tablespoons unsalted butter

Chopped chives, for garnish (optional)

Place the potatoes and garlic in a large saucepan, cover with cold water, and add a generous pinch of salt. Bring to a boil over high heat and cook until tender and easily pierced with a fork, 15 to 20 minutes.

Meanwhile, heat the milk and butter in a small saucepan over medium-low heat. Once the butter is melted, remove from the heat and set aside.

Drain the potatoes and return them to the pot. Mash the potatoes slightly, then add the butter and milk mixture. Mash until smooth, then season to taste with salt and pepper.

Transfer the mashed potatoes to a serving bowl and garnish with black pepper and chives (if desired).

Crispy Parmesan Potatoes

When these potatoes first showed up on my TikTok feed, I was intrigued. They looked so easy and delicious that I had to try them. After a few rounds of tinkering, I have simplified a nearly foolproof recipe with a *spudtacular* balance of saltiness and savory flavor, thanks to the Parmesan. The texture is addictive, soft and creamy on the inside and with a crispy exterior that's divine. A squeeze of fresh lemon juice can add a zing that takes this to the next level.

1 pound baby Dutch Yellow potatoes

½ stick (4 tablespoons) unsalted butter, melted

⅓ cup freshly grated Parmesan (about 1½ ounces)

1 teaspoon garlic powder

1 teaspoon dried oregano

Kosher salt and freshly ground black pepper

1 tablespoon extra virgin olive oil

Preheat the oven to 425°F.

Cut the potatoes in half lengthwise. Use a sharp knife to score the potatoes by cutting a ¼-inch-deep crosshatch pattern on the cut side of each potato half.

Using a silicone spatula, mix together the melted butter, Parmesan, garlic powder, oregano, and ½ teaspoon black pepper in a 9 × 13-inch baking dish until it creates a paste. Use the spatula to spread the cheese mixture into an even layer, completely covering the base of the pan.

Place the potatoes cut side down in the prepared baking dish. Try not to move the potatoes around once you get them in the dish. Use a pastry brush to brush the olive oil on the tops of the potatoes. Season the potato skins with a pinch of salt and pepper.

Bake for 20 to 30 minutes, until the potatoes are fork-tender and the Parmesan is crispy and browned.

Use a fork to remove the potatoes from the baking dish. The cut side of the potato should be crusted in the cheese. Transfer the potatoes to a serving platter and serve immediately.

Baked Sweet Potato Fries

I remember the first time I made sweet potato fries for my son and his friends. They were a bunch of middle school boys who wanted their French fries and weren't interested in trying something new. But they loved them, and I ended up making these on the regular as an after-school snack.

2 medium sweet potatoes, peeled and cut into even French fry shapes (slightly larger than ¼-inch batons)

2 tablespoons extra virgin olive oil

1 tablespoon cornstarch

½ teaspoon paprika

¼ teaspoon garlic powder

⅛ teaspoon cayenne pepper

Kosher salt and freshly ground black pepper

Classic Ranch Dressing (page 320)

Preheat the oven to 450°F.

Toss the sweet potatoes with the olive oil in a large bowl. Stir together the cornstarch, paprika, garlic powder, cayenne, ¾ teaspoon salt, and a few grinds of black pepper in a small bowl. Sprinkle the spice mixture over the sweet potatoes and toss to coat.

Arrange the sweet potatoes on a baking sheet in a single layer, leaving as much space between the fries as possible. Bake for 20 to 25 minutes, rotating the baking sheet once after about 15 minutes, until the edges are browned and crispy. Let cool for 5 minutes before serving.

Serve the warm fries with the ranch dressing.

> Indulge in your life.
> Indulge in yourself.
> You deserve it.

Baked Potato Chips

For those who don't want to pull out the deep fryer or mess with hot oil, bake 'em up.

1 medium russet potato, scrubbed clean

2 tablespoons extra virgin olive oil

For the Lemon Pepper Seasoning

2 teaspoons lemon pepper (salt-free), ground into a fine powder in a spice grinder

½ teaspoon kosher salt

For the BBQ Seasoning

½ teaspoon paprika

½ teaspoon powdered sugar

½ teaspoon kosher salt

¼ teaspoon onion powder

¼ teaspoon smoked paprika

¼ teaspoon chili powder

For the Celery Salt Seasoning

½ teaspoon dried parsley

½ teaspoon onion powder

½ teaspoon garlic powder

¼ teaspoon freshly ground black pepper

½ teaspoon celery salt

Additional Seasoning Options

2 teaspoons chicken salt

1 teaspoon finely ground smoked salt + ½ teaspoon freshly ground black pepper

Preheat the oven to 425°F. Line a baking sheet with parchment paper.

Use a mandoline or a very sharp knife to cut the potato into ⅛-inch slices. Arrange the potato slices on paper towels to remove any excess moisture.

Transfer the potato slices to a large bowl and add the olive oil and your seasoning of choice. Toss to evenly coat.

Place the potatoes in an even layer on the prepared baking sheet. You may need to use a second parchment-lined baking sheet, depending on the size of your potato.

Bake for 13 to 15 minutes, until the chips are golden and the edges are curling up. The chips may be slightly soft in the center but will continue to firm up as they cool. Feel free to sprinkle with a little extra salt, if desired.

Homemade Potato Chips with Chicken Salt

I have a friend who says, "Either you love potato chips or you're addicted to them." Exactly. The addition of chicken salt, a super-popular spice Down Under made with salt, paprika, garlic, and more, adds umami perfection. My favorite, Jada Spices, makes a vegan option that can be found online.

3 medium Yukon Gold
   potatoes
Vegetable oil, for frying
1 tablespoon chicken salt

Slice the potatoes about 1⁄16 inch thick on a mandoline. Put the potato slices in a large bowl of cold water and agitate the water to release the starch. Drain and repeat until the water remains clear, about three more times. Line two baking sheets with paper towels and spread the potatoes on top in a single layer; pat dry thoroughly.

Fill a large, wide pot with 2 inches of vegetable oil. Heat the oil to 315°F over medium-high heat. Fry a small batch of potatoes until golden brown and crispy, 3 to 4 minutes. Using a large slotted spoon, transfer the chips to a paper towel–lined pan and sprinkle with some of the chicken salt. Repeat with the remaining potatoes and chicken salt, returning the oil to temperature between batches.

Turkey Cottage Pie

PHOTO ON PAGE 219

I always thought this dish was traditional shepherd's pie, but while looking into the English side of my family tree, I discovered that it's properly called cottage pie when turkey is used instead of lamb. Whatever you call it, each sumptuous bite of this dish—turkey (the dark meat makes it super rich and moist and yummy) and mashed potatoes, with peas and carrots, all baked into a pie—gets to the very core of what it means to indulge in comfort food. This is an excellent choice for a family meal.

2 tablespoons unsalted butter

1 yellow onion, finely chopped

Kosher salt and freshly ground black pepper

1½ pounds ground dark meat turkey

2 teaspoons chopped thyme

4 garlic cloves, grated

2 tablespoons all-purpose flour

1¼ cups low-sodium chicken stock

1 tablespoon Worcestershire sauce

One 12-ounce bag frozen peas and carrots

4 cups Classic Mashed Potatoes (page 220)

¼ cup freshly grated Parmesan (about 1 ounce)

Chopped chives, for garnish

Preheat the oven to 400°F. Place a 9 × 13-inch baking dish on a baking sheet to avoid oven spills.

Melt the butter in a large nonstick skillet over medium-high heat. Add the onion and a pinch of salt and pepper. Cook, stirring occasionally, until the onion has softened, about 5 minutes. Increase the heat to medium-high and add the ground turkey. Season with 1 teaspoon salt and ½ teaspoon pepper. Cook, using a wooden spoon to break it into small pieces, until the turkey is browned, 5 to 7 minutes.

Add the thyme and garlic and cook just until the garlic is fragrant, 1 to 2 minutes. Sprinkle the flour over the meat mixture and stir until the flour has been absorbed and no white spots remain. Add the chicken stock and Worcestershire sauce and cook until the mixture has thickened, about 1 minute. Remove from the heat and stir in the peas and carrots. Season to taste with salt and pepper.

Transfer the mixture to the prepared baking dish. Dollop the mashed potatoes on top of the meat mixture and carefully spread it out to completely cover the meat. Top the mashed potatoes with the Parmesan and a sprinkle of pepper. Transfer the dish on the baking sheet to the oven and bake for 35 to 40 minutes, until the filling is bubbling. For a lightly browned, crispy crust, turn the broiler on for the last 2 minutes. Keep an eye on the cottage pie as it can brown very quickly.

Let sit for 10 minutes before serving. Garnish with chives.

The Best Bottle of Wine You'll Ever Have

Confession time: I wasn't yet ten years old when I had my first sip of wine, poured from a gallon bottle of chianti in my aunt Adeline's basement. Rather than scrunch up my face at the taste, I was the rare kid who said, "Does this wine need to breathe?" I'm kidding, of course, but it did start a lifelong passion for wine, and now, believe it or not, I am the proud owner of a vineyard right in my own backyard. When I step outside, I feel like I'm transported to the picturesque wine regions of Italy, France, or Napa. It's a luxury I never dreamed of, but when I moved into my home, the big, sloping hill in my backyard lacked vegetation and was prone to mudslides. A suggestion to plant grapes sparked the idea, and over ten years later, I now have a stunning vineyard that yields around two hundred bottles of merlot a year.

My younger self, lacking the appreciation I now have for the craft of winemaking, would be surprised to hear me say that learning more about wine is as enjoyable, if not more so, than savoring it. But it's true. It's made me a first-rate browser in the wine section at the grocery store, at my favorite wine shop, and when I'm handed a wine menu in a restaurant, all of which can be confusing and intimidating experiences. So what do you do? "Ask questions," says Los Angeles wine expert Taylor Grant, who was one of *Food & Wine* magazine's 2019 Sommeliers of the Year. "Take advantage of someone's expertise. When I worked in a restaurant, my favorite thing was being called over to a table, talking with someone about what they wanted—do they want to stick with what they like or branch out—having them try something, and creating that experience."

I sat down with Taylor over a pizza topped with mozzarella, Calabrese salami, and Castelvetrano olives. It was a little spicy. Taylor ordered an Etna Rosso, a red wine grown on Mount Etna, swirled it in her glass, then sniffed, as did I. "Cherry?" I said, slightly unsure of myself. "Exactly," Taylor said. "Strong wild cherry." Why did she select this wine? "The pizza has some spice to it, and a more acidic wine will stand up to it," she explained. Confidently pairing wine and food is an enviable skill. Though Taylor was reluctant to state hard-and-fast rules, she offered this generalization: try to match reds and contrast whites with the meal. Then she rattled off exceptions. For example, if you're making a pork chop with a chutney, you might want a white with a hint of sweetness. "You won't even notice the sweetness of the wine," she said. "But that's the point." The other point is there are no set rules.

It helps to know your way around pinots, burgundies, cabernets, chardonnays, sauvignon blancs, and Rieslings, but it's not essential, if you keep in mind, as I do, you're only a question away from picking a bottle that will enhance your meal—and that's key. My most memorable wine experience came at a tiny restaurant in San Gimignano, in Tuscany. My hotel sent me there. The owner was a character. I ordered lasagna, he picked the wine, and it was spectacular, though I don't know whether it was the wine or the lasagna or the owner talking about the wine that made it all so good and memorable. "It was all of the above," Taylor said when I recalled the story for her. She said her biggest indulgence is dinner with family and friends where "we have one of everything and lots of bottles on the table and good conversation."

I agree. The best bottle of wine you'll ever have will be the best not because of how much it costs or where it was made but because of the people with whom you share it.

SEAFOOD

"I'm still amazed that my dad took our whole family out to dinner, because my three brothers and I would inevitably play 'see food' at the table, knowing my dad couldn't get mad in a restaurant. We still do it. But what I have here is a very different seafood."

Blackened Catfish Sandwiches

Catfish cooks up easily, holds together in the pan, and has a ton of flavor. Enjoy this sandwich for dinner as an indulgent change of pace, though if you don't feel like a sandwich, you can also make delicious blackened catfish soft tacos. Top with my Jalapeño Ranch Dressing, and please don't forget the garlic chips, because they put the whole dish right over the top. Can you tell I love this one?

2 catfish fillets (1 to 1½ pounds)

2 teaspoons Cajun seasoning

2 tablespoons avocado oil

8 garlic cloves, thinly sliced

½ stick (4 tablespoons) unsalted butter, room temperature

4 potato burger buns

½ cup Jalapeño Ranch Dressing (page 320)

8 butter lettuce leaves

⅓ cup dill pickle chips

Pat the catfish fillets dry and cut each fillet in half to create four smaller pieces that will comfortably fit on the burger buns. Season both sides of the catfish with the Cajun seasoning and set aside.

Line a plate with paper towels. Add the avocado oil and sliced garlic to a cold large pan. Turn the heat to medium and cook, stirring frequently, until the garlic is beginning to turn lightly golden brown, about 2 minutes. Use a slotted spoon to transfer the garlic to the paper towel–lined plate. Set aside.

Increase the heat to high and transfer the catfish fillets to the hot pan. Cook until lightly charred, about 3 minutes. Flip and cook until the fish is fully cooked and flakes easily with a fork, an additional 3 to 4 minutes. Transfer to a plate.

Spread the butter on the cut sides of the buns. Heat a large nonstick skillet over medium-high heat. Place the buns in the pan, cut side down. Cook until lightly golden, 2 to 3 minutes.

To assemble the sandwiches, spread the jalapeño ranch on both cut sides of the bun. Place two lettuce leaves on each of the bottom buns. Top the lettuce with pickle chips and a piece of fish. Sprinkle the garlic chips on top of the fish. Sandwich with the top buns. Serve immediately.

Calabrian Chili Shrimp on Toast

With many fine restaurants featuring variations of "something delicious on toast," I picked up on the trend in my own kitchen. This is one of my favorites, especially when I want something light and bright during the summer. The tangy vinaigrette drizzled on top of the shrimp and avocado is absolutely divine.

8 ounces large shrimp, peeled and deveined

¼ cup plus 2 tablespoons Calabrian Chili Vinaigrette (page 328)

Extra virgin olive oil

Four ½-inch slices Italian bread

1 small avocado, sliced

Kosher salt and freshly ground black pepper

Lemon wedges, for serving

Toss the shrimp with ¼ cup of the vinaigrette in a medium bowl. Set aside while you toast the bread. Do not let the shrimp marinate for more than 10 to 15 minutes; the acid in the vinaigrette will begin to cook the shrimp.

Add enough olive oil to lightly coat the base of a nonstick skillet and heat over medium heat. When the oil is gently shimmering, add the bread in an even layer and cook until golden brown and crisp, about 2 minutes. Flip and cook until crispy on the other side, an additional 1 to 2 minutes. Remove from the heat and transfer the toast to a plate.

Use a paper towel to wipe out any excess oil from the pan. Return the pan to the stove and heat over medium heat. Add the shrimp and cook until the shrimp are pink and cooked through, about 4 minutes. Remove from the heat.

To assemble, shingle the avocado slices on the toast. Season the avocado with salt and pepper. Evenly divide the shrimp on top of the avocado. Drizzle with the remaining 2 tablespoons vinaigrette and serve with lemon wedges.

Chili Crisp Scallops and Corn

Once I got over my fear of scallops, which stemmed, embarrassingly enough, from not eating them, I learned just how delicious and versatile they are and how easy they are to make, and now I will regularly indulge in these gems. This dish takes no time to put together, and it's packed with intense flavor.

12 large scallops
   (approximately 1 pound)

Kosher salt and freshly
   ground black pepper

2 teaspoons chili crisp oil
   (page 330 or store-bought),
   plus more for garnish
   if desired

3 tablespoons unsalted butter

3 cups fresh sweet corn
   (from 4 ears)

Chopped chives, for garnish

Remove the muscle from the side of the scallops and pat them dry. Season both sides with salt and pepper.

Heat the chili crisp oil and 2 tablespoons of the butter in a large cast-iron skillet over medium-high heat. Once the butter is melted, add the scallops in an even layer and cook, undisturbed, until they release easily from the pan and have a nice crust, about 2 minutes. Flip and continue to cook until crisp and cooked through, an additional 2 to 3 minutes. Transfer to a plate and set aside.

Add the remaining 1 tablespoon butter to the hot pan. Once the butter is melted, add the corn and season with ½ teaspoon salt. Cook, stirring frequently, until the corn is crisp-tender, about 3 minutes.

Serve the scallops on top of the corn. Garnish with chives and more chili crisp (if desired).

Coconut Poached Salmon and Rice

Poaching salmon infuses it with flavor, but one day I wanted to indulge in a little extra oomph. In my previous cookbook, I had a recipe for coconut soup, which I adored, and I thought coconut milk would be great for poaching seafood. I was right. I started with clams, then tried salmon, and I have to tell you, it's divine.

1 stalk lemongrass

1 tablespoon coconut oil

½ yellow onion, thinly sliced

3 garlic cloves, sliced

1 tablespoon grated ginger

One 13.5-ounce can coconut milk

1 tablespoon red curry paste

1 tablespoon fish sauce

1 teaspoon lime zest

One 1-pound salmon fillet, skin and pin bones removed

Kosher salt and freshly ground black pepper

2 tablespoons freshly squeezed lime juice

1 cup jasmine rice

1 tablespoon unsalted butter

3 green onions, white and light green parts, sliced

Chopped cilantro, for garnish

Thai basil leaves, for garnish

To prepare the lemongrass, trim the top and the root end of the stalk, leaving yourself the center 4 inches. Remove any thick, woody outer layers. Place the stalk on a cutting board and use the dull side of your knife to bash it a few times to release the flavors. Set aside until ready to use.

Melt the coconut oil in a large straight-sided skillet over medium heat. Add the onion and cook, stirring occasionally, until translucent and soft, about 4 minutes. Add the garlic, ginger, and lemongrass and cook until just fragrant, about 1 minute. Add the coconut milk, red curry paste, fish sauce, and lime zest. Whisk to evenly combine. Bring the mixture up to a simmer, then reduce the heat to low.

Season the salmon with salt and pepper. Gently nestle it into the coconut broth and spoon some of the sauce and onions on top. Cover and cook on low until the salmon is cooked through and flakes easily with a fork, 15 to 20 minutes. Remove from the heat and add the lime juice.

Meanwhile, make the rice. Rinse the rice thoroughly in a fine-mesh strainer. Place it in a small saucepan with 2 cups of water. Add the butter and ½ teaspoon salt. Bring to a boil, stir the rice, reduce the heat to low, cover, and cook until all the water has been absorbed, 15 minutes. Remove the lid and add the green onions. Fluff with a fork. Cover and let sit until the salmon is ready.

To serve, divide the rice evenly among four bowls. Flake off large chunks of salmon and add it to the bowls with the rice, spooning over some of the coconut broth and onions. Garnish with cilantro and Thai basil.

Crispy Cod Sandwiches

When I used to drive carpools and had a full load of preteens in the back, I would sometimes pull into McDonald's after baseball or soccer practice. I always ordered the same thing, the Filet-O-Fish. This is my homage to Chef Mickey D's classic.

Cooking spray

1 cup all-purpose flour

Kosher salt and freshly ground black pepper

2 large eggs

½ cup panko bread crumbs

½ cup Italian-style bread crumbs

1 to 1½ pounds cod (about ¾ to 1 inch thick)

4 brioche burger buns

3 tablespoons unsalted butter, room temperature

⅓ cup Tartar Sauce (page 331 or store-bought)

4 slices American cheese

Preheat the oven to 400°F. Line a baking sheet with foil and set a wire rack inside. Spray the rack with cooking spray.

Set up your dredging station. Combine the flour, ½ teaspoon salt, and ¼ teaspoon pepper in a shallow bowl and mix with a fork. Whisk together the eggs in a separate shallow bowl. In a third shallow bowl, combine the panko and Italian bread crumbs with a fork.

Cut the cod into four equal pieces to fit your buns. Season both sides with salt and pepper. Working with one piece at a time, dredge the fish in the flour mixture, completely coating it. Tap off any excess. Next, dip the fish in the egg, coating it on both sides. Let any excess egg drip off, then transfer the fish to the bread crumb mixture. Turn the fish in the bread crumbs to completely coat it. Transfer to the prepared rack. Repeat with the remaining fish.

Once all of the fish has been coated, spray it liberally with cooking spray. Bake for 20 to 25 minutes, until the fish registers 145°F on an instant-read thermometer.

Meanwhile, cut the buns in half and spread the cut sides with the butter. Heat a large nonstick skillet over medium heat. Place the buns in the pan, cut side down, and cook until toasty and golden, 2 to 3 minutes. Transfer to a plate.

To assemble, spread the tartar sauce on both cut sides of the buns. Place a piece of fish on each bottom bun. Top with a piece of cheese. Sandwich with the top buns. Serve immediately.

Lemon Whitefish with Roasted Fennel Slaw

This elegant dish will make you feel like you went to cooking school. Whitefish is delicate, and something wonderful happens to it when it's baked in butter, garlic, lemon, and capers. The roasted fennel make it a full, flavorful meal. Pair with some Baby Kale with Crispy Garlic (page 151) or Blistered Green Beans (page 152), and you're in for a treat. Indulge!

3 small fennel bulbs

1 tablespoon extra virgin olive oil

Kosher salt and freshly ground black pepper

3 tablespoons unsalted butter

3 garlic cloves, grated

1 teaspoon lemon zest

2 tablespoons freshly squeezed lemon juice

1 tablespoon drained capers

1 to 1½ pounds whitefish, cut into 4 equal fillets

Preheat the oven to 400°F. Line a baking sheet with parchment paper.

Trim the fennel and reserve ¼ cup of the fronds. Cut the bulbs in half, leaving the core intact. Cut each half into four wedges. Place the fennel in a large bowl and drizzle with the olive oil, ½ teaspoon salt, and ¼ teaspoon pepper. Toss to coat. Transfer to the prepared baking sheet and spread out in an even layer. Roast for 20 minutes.

Meanwhile, melt the butter in a small saucepan over medium-low heat. Once the butter is melted, remove from the heat and stir in the garlic, lemon zest, 1 tablespoon of the lemon juice, and the capers. Set aside.

Pat the fish dry and season both sides with salt and pepper.

Remove the baking sheet from the oven. Use a spatula to toss the fennel and move it over to one-half of the baking sheet. Add the whitefish to the empty side of the pan. Spoon the lemon-butter mixture over the fish. Return the pan to the oven to roast for 10 to 12 minutes, until the fish is cooked through and flakes easily with a fork.

Transfer the fennel to a cutting board. Roughly chop it and add to a bowl. Roughly chop the reserved fronds and add them to the bowl along with the remaining 1 tablespoon lemon juice. Toss to combine.

To serve, plate the fennel slaw alongside the fish.

Salmon Burgers with Quick-Pickled Vegetables

I'll tell you paradise: a salmon burger, a glass of white wine, and a seat on the patio as the sun sets on a warm summer night. Next time the urge for a hamburger strikes, try indulging in a salmon burger instead. Make the quick-pickled veggies ahead to give them at least an hour to cool completely.

For the Quick-Pickled Vegetables

1½ cups distilled white vinegar

2 teaspoons pickling spice

½ teaspoon kosher salt

2 Persian cucumbers, sliced into ⅛-inch rounds

1 carrot, sliced into ⅛-inch rounds

1 shallot, sliced into ⅛-inch rings

1 Fresno chile, sliced into ⅛-inch rings

For the Burgers

4 green onions, roughly chopped

1 red bell pepper, roughly chopped

One 2-inch piece ginger, peeled and roughly chopped

1 garlic clove, roughly chopped

1 tablespoon lime zest (from 1 to 2 limes)

1 pound salmon, skin removed, cut into 1½-inch cubes

1¼ cups panko bread crumbs

1 bunch cilantro, stems chopped (about ¼ cup) and leaves with tender stems reserved to top the burgers

1 tablespoon sweet chili sauce

1 teaspoon toasted sesame oil

1 tablespoon low-sodium soy sauce

Cooking spray

2 tablespoons vegetable oil

6 oblong brioche buns, sliced in half horizontally

⅓ cup mayonnaise

To make the quick-pickled vegetables, combine the vinegar, ½ cup of water, pickling spice, and salt in a small saucepan. Bring the mixture to a simmer over medium heat, then remove from the heat and add the cucumbers, carrot, shallot, and chile. Let cool completely. Refrigerate in an airtight container for up to 5 days.

To make the burgers, combine the green onions, bell pepper, ginger, garlic, and lime zest in a food processor. Pulse until the vegetables are finely chopped. Add the salmon, panko, cilantro stems, sweet chili sauce, sesame oil, and soy sauce. Pulse to roughly chop the salmon and incorporate it into the vegetable mixture. The mixture should be chunky, not a paste. Lightly coat clean hands with cooking spray and form six patties, about ½ cup each, the same shape and size as the buns.

Heat a large nonstick skillet over medium-high heat. Add the vegetable oil and swirl to coat the pan. Add the patties and cook until the internal temperature reaches 145°F on an instant-read thermometer, about 4 minutes per side.

To assemble the burgers, lay the buns cut side up on a clean work surface. Spread mayo on both sides of the buns. Place a salmon patty on each bun and top with pickled veggies and cilantro leaves.

Seafood Rolls

Lobster rolls were a summer treat when I was a little kid growing up in Delaware. But I made this twist on the classic because Wolfie loves crab, his wife loves shrimp, and I still can't get enough lobster. The recipe works for any type of seafood; I made crab for Wolfie, shrimp for Andraia, and lobster for me when they came over for dinner one day last summer. You can also get crazy and *combine* all three!

1 pound cooked shrimp (or lobster or crab), cut into bite-size pieces*

1 large celery stalk, chopped

3 green onions, thinly sliced

1 tablespoon chopped chives

1 teaspoon chopped dill

2 teaspoons lemon zest

1 tablespoon freshly squeezed lemon juice

½ teaspoon garlic powder

½ teaspoon seafood seasoning, such as Old Bay

⅓ cup mayonnaise

Kosher salt and freshly ground black pepper

Toasted split-top buns

Potato chips (page 227 or store-bought), for serving (optional)

*Feel free to substitute jumbo lump crab meat or cooked chopped lobster for the shrimp or get ⅓ pound each for a blend of all three.

Combine the shrimp, celery, green onions, chives, dill, lemon zest and juice, garlic powder, seafood seasoning, and mayo in a large bowl. Carefully fold the mixture together, using a silicone spatula, until evenly incorporated. Season to taste with salt and pepper.

Spoon the shrimp mixture into toasted buns and serve immediately with potato chips (if desired).

Seafood Tomato Sauce with Crusty Bread

My brother David would make this after we got back from a day of skiing in Park City, Utah. Impressed that he came up with it, I would take a bite and literally my eyes would shut and my tired and achy body would say, *Thank you*. A lot of that had to do with the crusty bread. I've tweaked the sauce over the years. It's just great flavors all together, and it's also delicious served over pasta.

2 tablespoons extra virgin olive oil

8 ounces large shrimp, peeled and deveined, roughly chopped

6 ounces bay scallops

Kosher salt and freshly ground black pepper

2 garlic cloves, sliced

¼ cup dry white wine

One 28-ounce can crushed tomatoes

2 tablespoons chopped parsley

1 bay leaf

½ teaspoon cayenne pepper

½ teaspoon dried oregano

One 6-ounce can chopped clams, drained

Crusty bread, for serving

Heat the olive oil in a large straight-sided skillet over medium heat. Once the oil is shimmering, add the shrimp and scallops. Season with salt and pepper. Cook, stirring frequently, until the shrimp is pink and the scallops are cooked through, about 5 minutes. Transfer to a plate and set aside.

Add the garlic to the pan and cook until soft and fragrant, about 2 minutes. Pour in the wine to deglaze the pan, scraping up any browned bits from the bottom of the pan. Cook until the harsh alcohol smell burns off, about 2 minutes. Add the crushed tomatoes, parsley, bay leaf, cayenne, oregano, and ½ teaspoon salt. Bring the mixture to a boil, then reduce the heat to low, cover, and simmer for 20 minutes.

After 20 minutes, add the clams and cooked shrimp and scallops. Stir to combine. Cook until the seafood is heated through, about 5 minutes. Remove from the heat and discard the bay leaf. Season to taste with salt and pepper.

Let cool for 5 minutes before serving with crusty bread.

Shrimp and Veggie Lettuce Cups

I can picture myself at twenty years old, watching Mrs. Van Halen cook in her Pasadena kitchen and asking her about this ingredient and that as she cooked up her version of this dish. She cooked without recipes, putting a little of this and a little of that in her wok. I like a recipe, though, and this is truly a good one with crunch, sweetness, and tang—all the tastes and textures I love.

3 tablespoons tamari or low-sodium soy sauce

1 tablespoon hoisin sauce

1 tablespoon rice vinegar

½ teaspoon toasted sesame oil

2 teaspoons Easy Garlic Chili Crisp (page 330 or store-bought chili crisp)

1 tablespoon grated ginger

3 garlic cloves, grated

1 teaspoon cornstarch

2 tablespoons coconut oil

12 ounces shrimp, peeled, deveined, then sliced in half lengthwise

Kosher salt and freshly ground black pepper

1 red bell pepper, diced

3 ounces snap peas, thinly sliced

4 green onions, cut into 1-inch pieces

½ cup pineapple, finely diced

⅓ cup sliced water chestnuts, drained and cut into matchsticks

Butter lettuce leaves, for serving

⅓ cup carrot matchsticks, for garnish

Cilantro leaves, for garnish

Thai basil, for garnish

Whisk together the tamari, hoisin, rice vinegar, sesame oil, chili crisp, ginger, garlic, and cornstarch in a small bowl. Set aside.

Heat 1 tablespoon of the coconut oil in a large nonstick skillet over medium-high heat. Once the oil is shimmering, add the shrimp and season with salt and pepper. Cook, stirring occasionally, until the shrimp is pink and cooked through, 4 to 5 minutes. Transfer to a plate and set aside.

Add the remaining 1 tablespoon coconut oil to the pan. Add the bell pepper, snap peas, and green onions. Cook, stirring occasionally, until the vegetables have softened, about 5 minutes. Add the pineapple and water chestnuts to the vegetable mixture and cook until just heated through, about 2 minutes. Add the shrimp back to the pan along with the sauce. Stir to coat the vegetables and shrimp in the sauce. Cook until the sauce has slightly thickened, about 2 minutes. Remove from the heat.

To assemble, spoon the shrimp mixture into the lettuce cups. Top with carrot matchsticks, cilantro, and Thai basil. Serve immediately.

Chipotle Shrimp Salad Lettuce Cups

I like turning simple into fancy. Presentation is important and is another way to indulge yourself and others. This zesty shrimp salad is a perfect example. It looks elegant on the plate and tastes refreshingly sublime. A guaranteed smile, even if it's just you at the table.

⅓ cup mayonnaise

2 to 3 teaspoons chopped chipotles in adobo (depending on desired spice level)

1 tablespoon chopped cilantro, plus whole leaves for garnish if desired

½ teaspoon lime zest

½ teaspoon ground cumin

Kosher salt

12 ounces frozen cooked salad shrimp, thawed and well drained

1 celery stalk, finely chopped

½ cup finely chopped red bell pepper

1 small Persian cucumber, finely chopped

½ avocado, sliced

1 head butter lettuce, broken into leaves

Lime wedges, for serving

Combine the mayo, chipotles, cilantro, lime zest, cumin, and ½ teaspoon of salt in a large bowl. Add the drained shrimp, celery, bell pepper, and cucumber to the dressing and mix gently to combine.

To assemble, place the sliced avocado in the lettuce cups and season lightly with salt. Top the avocado with shrimp salad and garnish with cilantro leaves, if desired. Serve with lime wedges.

Smoky Slow-Roasted Cod Puttanesca

I know puttanesca is delicious over pasta, but when you roast a nice piece of cod in it, the fish is just crazy good. You could whip up some pasta or rice on the side, but I generally make a Caesar salad and savor all the big flavors.

2 teaspoons smoked paprika

1 teaspoon Italian seasoning

1 teaspoon garlic powder

1 teaspoon onion powder

½ teaspoon red pepper flakes

Kosher salt

One 1- to 1½-pound cod fillet

¼ cup extra virgin olive oil

One 14.5-ounce can diced tomatoes

½ cup roughly chopped roasted red peppers

1 shallot, sliced into rings

2 garlic cloves, grated

½ cup pitted Castelvetrano olives, halved

2 tablespoons drained capers

1 tablespoon chopped oregano

1 tablespoon chopped parsley, plus whole leaves for garnish

1 teaspoon lemon zest

Basil leaves, for garnish

Lemon wedges, for serving

Preheat the oven to 350°F.

Stir together the smoked paprika, Italian seasoning, garlic powder, onion powder, pepper flakes, and 1½ teaspoons salt in a small bowl.

Pat the fish dry and season on both sides with 3 teaspoons of the spice mixture. Set aside.

Combine the olive oil, tomatoes, roasted red peppers, shallot, garlic, olives, capers, oregano, parsley, and lemon zest in a 9 × 13-inch baking dish. Add the remaining seasoning mix and stir to combine. Nestle the seasoned cod into the sauce.

Bake for 25 to 30 minutes, until the cod is cooked through and flakes easily with a fork. Garnish with parsley and basil leaves. Serve with lemon wedges.

PASTA

"I grew up with pasta. It's in my DNA . . . and I'm done feeling guilty about it."

Creamy No-Cream Artichoke Pasta

I am eating in more of a plant-based direction, and this is one of those dishes that gets more vegetables and fiber into my diet. I love the way blending the artichoke hearts, olive oil, garlic, and other seasonings turns this into a no-cream cream sauce. For your gluten-free friends, make this with zoodles.

1 pound fettuccine

Two 14-ounce cans artichoke hearts, drained

Kosher salt and freshly ground black pepper

2 tablespoons extra virgin olive oil, plus more for garnish

4 garlic cloves, thinly sliced

½ teaspoon red pepper flakes

1 cup chopped roasted red peppers

½ cup pitted kalamata olives, halved

3 tablespoons drained capers

¼ cup chopped parsley

¼ cup chopped basil

Bring a large pot of salted water to a boil. Add the pasta to the water and cook until al dente according to the package directions. Reserve 1 cup of pasta water and transfer the pasta to a colander to drain.

Meanwhile, combine the artichoke hearts, ¼ cup of water, ¼ teaspoon salt, and ¼ teaspoon black pepper in a high-powered blender and blend on medium until completely smooth. Set aside.

Heat a large straight-sided skillet over medium heat. Add the olive oil, garlic, pepper flakes, and roasted red peppers. Cook, stirring frequently, until the garlic is slightly softened but not browned, about 1 to 2 minutes. Add the olives, capers, and blended artichoke hearts. Stir to combine and reduce the heat to low.

Add the drained pasta directly to the pan with the artichoke sauce. Pour in about ½ cup of the reserved pasta water and toss until the pasta water and artichoke sauce become a cohesive creamy mixture, adding more pasta water if needed to reach the desired consistency. Remove from the heat. Add the parsley and basil and toss to combine.

Serve topped with extra freshly ground black pepper and a drizzle of olive oil.

Four-Cheese Baked Ziti

Go ahead, indulge in this classic baked pasta dish. I turn to it especially when I've got leftover pasta or when I don't want to go through the effort of making a lasagna but still crave the comfort of all that flavor out of the oven.

Cooking spray

1 pound ziti

2 cups freshly grated provolone piccante (about 8 ounces)

1 cup freshly grated low-moisture mozzarella (about 4 ounces)

1 large egg

15 ounces ricotta

3 garlic cloves, grated

One 10-ounce package frozen spinach, thawed and thoroughly drained

2 tablespoons chopped basil

Kosher salt and freshly ground black pepper

One 32-ounce jar marinara sauce

2 teaspoons Calabrian chili paste

½ cup freshly grated Parmesan (about 2 ounces)

Preheat the oven to 425°F. Spray a 9 × 13-inch baking dish with cooking spray.

Bring a large pot of salted water to a boil. Add the pasta to the water and cook according to the package directions. Reserve ½ cup of the pasta water and transfer the pasta to a colander to drain.

Meanwhile, toss the provolone and mozzarella in a medium bowl; set aside until ready to assemble. Whisk the egg in a medium bowl to break up the yolk. Add the ricotta, garlic, spinach, basil, ½ teaspoon salt, and ¼ teaspoon pepper to the bowl with the egg and mix to evenly combine. Set aside.

Transfer the drained pasta back into the pot and add the reserved pasta water, marinara sauce, chili paste, and ¼ cup of the Parmesan. Toss to evenly coat the noodles in the sauce.

To assemble, layer half of the pasta mixture in the prepared baking dish. Dollop half of the ricotta mixture over the noodles. Top the ricotta with half of the mozzarella-provolone blend. Top the cheese with the remaining pasta. Dollop the remaining ricotta mixture on top of the noodles. Top with the remaining cheese blend and remaining ¼ cup Parmesan.

Bake for 25 to 30 minutes, until the sauce is bubbling and the cheese is melted and slightly browned in places. Let stand for 5 minutes before serving.

Lazy No-Bake Lasagna

My friend Rachael Ray has inspired me in countless ways, not least of which is trying to get dinner ready in 30 minutes, and this is one of those dishes. Frankly, sometimes you just don't have the hours it takes to make lasagna. This is quick and easy, and you get all the flavors of lasagna in one pan.

1 tablespoon extra virgin olive oil

1 pound bulk mild Italian sausage

2 cups Marinara Sauce (page 335 or store-bought)

12 ounces farfalle or mafaldine corte

8 ounces mini mozzarella balls

¾ cup ricotta

¼ cup freshly grated Parmesan (about 1 ounce)

Torn basil leaves, for garnish

Heat the olive oil in a Dutch oven or large, wide pot over medium-high heat. Add the sausage and cook, breaking up any clumps with a wooden spoon, until browned, about 6 minutes.

Add the marinara and 3½ cups of water to the pot with the sausage and bring the mixture to a boil.

Add the pasta, then partially cover and cook, stirring occasionally, until the pasta is al dente and the sauce is coating it nicely, about 16 minutes. Stir in the mozzarella and ricotta, then sprinkle with the Parmesan and basil, and serve.

Roasted Broccoli and Garlic Pasta

This dish was a staple of mine when Wolfie was a little kid and I was trying to get him to eat his veggies. Now I am the one who craves it. The little extra time it takes to roast the broccoli is worth it. It amplifies the flavor without any real effort.

1 pound broccoli crowns

6 tablespoons extra virgin olive oil

Kosher salt and freshly ground black pepper

1 pound fusilli

½ stick (4 tablespoons) unsalted butter

5 garlic cloves, sliced

½ cup freshly grated Parmesan (about 2 ounces), plus more for garnish

Preheat the oven to 400°F.

Cut the broccoli crowns into bite-size pieces. Trim the outer woody layer of the broccoli stem and slice it into coins. Place the broccoli on a baking sheet. Drizzle with 4 tablespoons of the olive oil and sprinkle with 1 teaspoon salt and ¼ teaspoon pepper. Toss to coat. Roast for 15 to 20 minutes, until the broccoli is tender and slightly browned.

Bring a large pot of salted water to a boil. Add the pasta to the water and cook until al dente according to the package directions. Reserve 1 cup of pasta water and transfer the pasta to a colander to drain.

Meanwhile, heat the butter and remaining 2 tablespoons olive oil in a large skillet over medium heat. Once the butter has melted, add the garlic and cook, stirring frequently, until fragrant and beginning to brown, about 2 minutes. Add ½ cup of the reserved pasta water and stir to combine. Add the drained pasta and the Parmesan to the pan with the garlic-butter mixture. Stir until the cheese is melted, adding up to ½ cup more pasta water if needed. Add the roasted broccoli and toss to combine. Season to taste with salt and pepper.

Serve in bowls and top with extra Parmesan and pepper.

Shrimp Scampi Pasta with Herb Bread Crumbs

My daughter-in-law adores shrimp, and I am constantly brainstorming new ways to prepare it. However, her favorite is the classic shrimp scampi served over pasta, and I take great pleasure in indulging her with this dish. The pasta is cooked to perfection, and the bread crumbs become even more delicious as they absorb the flavors of the butter, garlic, and white wine.

For the Topping

2 tablespoons unsalted butter

2 cups panko bread crumbs

2 tablespoons finely chopped chives

2 teaspoons finely chopped oregano

½ teaspoon lemon zest

Kosher salt

For the Pasta

2 tablespoons extra virgin olive oil

2 pounds large shrimp, peeled and deveined

Kosher salt and freshly ground black pepper

12 garlic cloves, finely chopped

1 shallot, finely chopped

1 cup dry white wine

¼ cup freshly squeezed lemon juice (from 1 to 2 lemons)

Red pepper flakes

Dried oregano

½ stick (4 tablespoons) unsalted butter, cut into chunks

¾ cup loosely packed fresh flat-leaf parsley, chopped

12 ounces capellini

Bring a large pot of salted water to a boil.

To make the topping, heat the butter in a large skillet over medium heat until melted and slightly browned but not burned. Add the bread crumbs. Using a wooden spoon, stir to coat the bread crumbs with the brown butter and toast until golden brown, 2 to 3 minutes. Remove from the heat. Stir in the chives, oregano, and lemon zest. Season to taste with salt and set aside.

To make the pasta, heat the oil in a large skillet over high heat. Season the shrimp all over with salt and pepper. Once the oil is shimmering, add the shrimp to the pan in an even layer and cook for 1 minute. Flip and cook for 1 more minute. Using a slotted spoon, transfer the shrimp to a bowl.

Add the garlic and shallot to the pan that held the shrimp and cook for 1 minute. Add the wine, lemon juice, and a pinch of pepper flakes and dried oregano and simmer for 3 minutes. Whisk in the butter piece by piece, thoroughly incorporating each piece before adding the next. Taste and season with salt and pepper as needed. Add the shrimp back to the pan and simmer until completely cooked through, about 2 minutes. Stir in the parsley. Remove from the heat.

Add the capellini to the boiling water and cook until just tender, about 4 minutes. Reserve 1 cup of the cooking water and transfer the capellini to a colander to drain. Toss the capellini with the shrimp and parsley, adding some of the pasta water if necessary to keep it moist. Transfer to a large serving bowl or into individual bowls and top with herb bread crumbs.

Spaghetti al Limone

Spaghetti and lemon might seem like an odd couple, but as far as I'm concerned, lemons go with everything. This recipe is a slight variation on the classic, and it still has all the amazing flavor of the butter, cheese, and lemon, making for a very special and easy meal. While it's not included in this recipe, I sometimes mix in thawed frozen peas before serving.

1 pound spaghetti

6 tablespoons unsalted butter, cut into cubes

2 garlic cloves, minced

1 tablespoon lemon zest

Kosher salt and freshly ground black pepper

2 tablespoons freshly squeezed lemon juice

⅓ cup freshly grated Parmesan (about 1½ ounces), plus more for serving

Bring a large pot of salted water to a boil. Add the pasta to the water and cook until al dente according to the package directions. Reserve 1 cup of pasta water and transfer the pasta to a colander to drain.

While the pasta is cooking, melt the butter in a large straight-sided skillet over medium-low heat. Add the garlic, lemon zest, and ¾ teaspoon salt. Cook until the garlic is fragrant but not yet golden, 1 to 2 minutes.

Add ½ cup of the reserved pasta water and the lemon juice to the butter mixture and stir to combine. Add the drained pasta and increase the heat to medium. Stir the mixture together in a circular motion until the sauce starts to emulsify and slightly thicken. This could take 2 to 3 minutes. When the sauce is shiny and glossy and sticking to the pasta, add the Parmesan and the remaining ½ cup pasta water. Stir again in a circular motion until the cheese melts and the sauce is glossy. Be patient, this could take a few minutes. Divide the pasta into bowls and spoon any remaining sauce over the pasta. Top with pepper and Parmesan. Serve immediately.

Spaghetti and Meatballs

I'm smiling right now as I remember all the times as a kid when I asked what we were having for dinner and my mom said, "Spaghetti and meatballs." If you're like me, this standard should be your first stop when you want to indulge in the comfort of such memories. I also believe this can be a wildly unexpected, elegant, and tasty meal when you have family or friends over for a special occasion.

For the Meatballs

1 pound ground beef

8 ounces bulk hot Italian sausage

1 large egg

2 garlic cloves, grated

½ cup Italian-style bread crumbs

¼ cup freshly grated Parmesan (about 1 ounce)

1 teaspoon kosher salt

½ teaspoon freshly ground black pepper

Extra virgin olive oil

For the Sauce

2 tablespoons extra virgin olive oil

4 garlic cloves, grated

One 28-ounce can crushed tomatoes

1 teaspoon Italian seasoning

¼ teaspoon red pepper flakes (optional)

1 large basil sprig

Kosher salt

1 pound spaghetti

6 tablespoons unsalted butter

¼ cup freshly grated Parmesan (about 1 ounce), plus more for garnish

To make the meatballs, combine the ground beef, sausage, egg, garlic, bread crumbs, Parmesan, salt, and pepper in a large bowl. Using clean hands or a silicone spatula, mix until the ingredients are evenly combined. Use a 3-tablespoon scoop or a ¼-cup measuring cup to scoop out a portion of the meat mixture. Roll the mixture into a ball and place on a plate. Repeat with the remaining mixture.

Bring a large pot of salted water to a boil.

Heat a large Dutch oven over medium-high heat. Add a few tablespoons of olive oil to lightly coat the base of the pan. Once the oil is shimmering, add the meatballs in an even layer. Be sure not to overcrowd the pan and give yourself enough space to be able to turn the meatballs; you may need to work in batches. Sear the meatballs on all sides, then transfer them to a plate. No need to cook them through at this step; they will finish cooking in the sauce. Feel free to add more oil if the pan seems dry between batches. Once all the meatballs are seared, set them aside and reduce the heat to medium-low.

To make the sauce, add the olive oil and garlic to the Dutch oven. Cook, stirring frequently, until the garlic is fragrant and lightly golden. This should only take a few seconds as the pan will be very hot. Add the tomatoes and stir to combine. Add ⅓ cup of water to the tomato can and swirl to remove any excess tomato from the sides of the can. Add the water to the pan with the tomato sauce. Stir in the Italian seasoning, pepper flakes (if using), basil sprig, and ½ teaspoon salt. Stir to combine and bring the sauce to a simmer. Add the meatballs back to the pan and turn them to coat them in the sauce. Reduce the heat to low and cover the pan. Cook, stirring and turning the meatballs occasionally, until cooked through, 10 to 15 minutes. Season to taste with salt.

While the meatballs are cooking, add the pasta to the boiling water and cook until al dente according to package directions. Drain and return to the pot. Add the butter and Parmesan and toss to combine.

Divide the spaghetti among the bowls and spoon the sauce and meatballs on top. Garnish with Parmesan.

Vegetable Bolognese with Spaghetti Squash

A *New York Times* article from years ago comparing the strands of spaghetti squash to angel hair pasta convinced me to try it, and I've been a fan ever since. Use this winter vegetable as you would any pasta and get the added nutritional benefits. This is my favorite way to use it, and even though I've rolled my eyes when people tell me that I won't miss the meat in their meatless Bolognese, I've turned into one of those people. Trust me, you really won't miss the meat in this Bolognese.

One 3- to 4-pound spaghetti squash

Extra virgin olive oil

Kosher salt and freshly ground black pepper

4 garlic cloves, roughly chopped

1 large carrot, roughly chopped

1 celery stalk, roughly chopped

1 large yellow onion, roughly chopped

1 pound cremini mushrooms, quartered

1 large zucchini, roughly chopped

½ cup milk

¾ cup dry red wine, such as pinot noir

One 28-ounce can crushed tomatoes

½ cup basil leaves, torn, plus more for serving

½ teaspoon red pepper flakes

One 2- to 3-ounce piece Parmesan rind plus freshly grated Parmesan, for serving

Preheat the oven to 400°F. Line a baking sheet with parchment paper.

Cut the spaghetti squash in half from top to bottom. Scoop out and discard the seeds. Place the squash cut side up on the prepared baking sheet. Drizzle each half with about 1½ teaspoons olive oil and season with a generous pinch of salt and black pepper. Turn the squash cut side down and bake for 40 minutes, or until a fork easily pulls the "spaghetti" strands away from the squash.

Meanwhile, start the sauce. Combine the garlic, carrot, celery, and onion in a food processor and pulse until the vegetables are finely chopped. Heat a Dutch oven or large pot over medium heat and add enough olive oil to coat the base of the pot, about 2 tablespoons. Add the chopped vegetables to the pot and season with ½ teaspoon each salt and black pepper. Cook, stirring occasionally, until the vegetables soften, about 5 minutes. Reattach the food processor bowl and add the mushrooms and zucchini. Pulse until the vegetables are finely chopped but still have some texture. Add them to the pot with the other vegetables. Season with another ½ teaspoon each salt and black pepper. Cook, stirring occasionally, until the vegetables are soft and their natural liquid has mostly evaporated, 7 to 10 minutes.

Add the milk to the pot and cook, stirring occasionally, until mostly evaporated, about 5 minutes. Next, pour in the red wine and cook, stirring occasionally, until the wine is mostly evaporated, about 7 minutes.

Add the crushed tomatoes, basil, pepper flakes, cheese rind, and ½ teaspoon salt to the pot. Bring the sauce up to a low boil, then

Feel free to use pasta instead of spaghetti squash if you prefer! Cook 1 pound of pasta according to the package directions and top with the sauce.

reduce the heat to low, cover, and simmer for 15 minutes. Remove the lid and let the sauce simmer uncovered for an additional 15 minutes. Remove and discard the cheese rind. Season the sauce with salt and pepper to taste.

To serve, add spaghetti squash to individual bowls and top with a big ladle of sauce, Parmesan, and torn basil.

Vongole with Sausage and Greens

When I get a craving for pasta vongole, I sometimes stray from the traditional recipe, and this is the result of one of those times. Adding sausage and greens makes this a hearty and full meal that hits all the right notes. The short wait between when the pan is covered and the clams open is like anticipating a first kiss at the end of a good date.

2 pounds littleneck or manila clams

Extra virgin olive oil

3 hot Italian sausage links (about 10 ounces), casings removed

2 shallots, sliced into rings

5 garlic cloves, chopped

¾ cup dry white wine, such as sauvignon blanc

1 pound fettuccine

1 bunch lacinato kale, ribs removed, thinly sliced

2 tablespoons freshly squeezed lemon juice

Kosher salt and freshly ground black pepper

2 tablespoons chopped parsley, for garnish

Lemon wedges, for serving

Soak the clams in cold water to purge any sand or impurities, 30 to 45 minutes. Drain well and set aside.

Bring a large pot of salted water to a boil.

Heat 1 tablespoon of olive oil in a large high-sided pan over medium-high heat. Add the sausage to the pan and cook, breaking it up with a wooden spoon, until browned and cooked through, 5 to 7 minutes. Use a slotted spoon to transfer the sausage to a plate and set aside.

If the pan looks dry after removing the sausage, add another tablespoon of olive oil. Add the shallot to the pan and cook until slightly softened, about 3 minutes. Add the garlic and cook until fragrant, about 1 minute. Pour in the wine to deglaze the pan, scraping up any browned bits from the bottom of the pan. Once the wine starts to simmer, reduce the heat to medium-low and add the clams. Cover and cook until the clams have opened, 10 to 15 minutes. Transfer the clams to a plate and set aside. Discard any clams that haven't opened.

Meanwhile, add the fettuccini to the boiling water and cook until al dente according to the package directions. Transfer to a colander to drain.

Add the kale and lemon juice to the pan where you cooked the clams and cook on medium-low heat until bright green and tender, about 3 minutes. Add the drained pasta and the sausage to the pan and toss to combine. Season to taste with salt and pepper. Top with parsley and clams and serve with lemon wedges. Serve immediately.

Good Show, Ma?

I cry easily. Most everyone who knows me is aware of this fact. I also laugh just as easily. And loudly. I've been told that my laugh is too loud. Laughs are like fingerprints. Everyone has a unique one. Most times, I can't really control how loudly I laugh, nor would I want to stifle my reaction to something that's funny. I mean, thank goodness I laugh. I wish I heard more laughter throughout the day, at any volume. Babies laughing, kids laughing, little old ladies laughing, strangers laughing. I love all of it. The world needs more laughter, if you ask me.

I also shout sometimes. I don't know if the world needs more of me shouting, but whenever people on super-loud motorcycles or cars speed down the street, their engines popping and exploding at ear-splitting decibels, I shout things at them. Sometimes awful, stupid things. Sometimes I'm shocked at the words that come out of my mouth.

My tears are different. For so many years, I didn't cry often enough because I tried so hard to stifle my feelings. I ate my emotions. I didn't want to feel anything bad or upsetting. Getting on a scale only contributed to this mindset. Every time I failed to hit my goal, whatever that goal happened to be at the time, it just confirmed that I was a failure, and it numbed me to feeling anything positive about myself. It was only when I said, "Enough already," and decided I wanted more joy in my life that I realized I couldn't experience joy without opening myself up to sadness and pain. I had to be emotionally honest.

My divorce followed. Ed passed away. And I cried. For three years. It was the great flood. Biblical in proportion. There were gushers every day. But it was also very cleansing. Because the flip side was the joy I had blocked out even more than the sadness. When Wolfie's first album was released, I cried. When he was nominated for a Grammy Award, more tears. When he told me that he was going to propose to his girlfriend, Andraia, I wept. When they called to report that she'd said yes, I screamed— and then I cried. And more recently, when the two of them invited me to their house to taste the food they were choosing for their wedding, I said I would be honored. Then I hung up the phone and bawled.

Why was I crying when I was happy? *This was joy,* I told myself. Never would I have thought I'd sail there on a river of tears.

It was strange. The more I let myself cry, the better I felt. I wasn't sad. I was happy. I wasn't thin. But I wasn't trying to be anything other than who I was, and if I happened to lose weight in the process of feeling good, all the better. I would get wherever it was I was supposed to be at age sixty-three. *Give it time,* I told myself. As the days turned into weeks and then months, I noticed that I no longer felt the need to stuff myself with food. I drank much less, if at all. I took long walks every day, savoring the steps, the sun and fresh air, and the thumping of my heartbeat. If I felt angsty or angry or scared or sad, I didn't ignore those feelings or try to tamp them down with food. I embraced them. I examined why I felt that way, and if I couldn't figure it out on my own, I got help.

A friend and I went out for dinner to an old-fashioned steak restaurant not too far from where I live. I had gone there many times over the years but always avoided their famous garlic cheese bread and felt guilty for everything I did eat. This time, though, I enjoyed one slice of the garlic cheese bread, and when I had my fill of steak and broccoli, I stopped and took the rest home. I ate—and enjoyed! For dessert, my friend ordered a slice of carrot cake while I declined, explaining it was a funny thing with me and dessert.

I do have a sweet tooth. I love anything with lemon. I also love holiday cookies, pumpkin pies, fruit tarts, and occasionally a hot fudge sundae with whipped cream, salty peanuts, and cherries. But I am not always in the mood. That's a big change for me. In the past, I was always in the mood. Not necessarily for dessert as much as I craved something sweet. I had a candy drawer in the kitchen. Then one day I tossed out everything in the drawer and replaced it with granola, chia seeds, and protein bars. The bars are still there. I craved a different kind of sweet.

I got a taste of it the day I went to Wolfie's to sample the wedding menu. When I walked into the kitchen, the caterer's chef was busy making the food, which smelled phenomenal. Wolfie and Andraia were in the dining room. The table was set the way the tables would look out in the backyard the night of the wedding. The tablecloths were beautiful. The place settings were elegant. Candles were lit. I couldn't believe how beautiful it looked, and there was my son with his bride-to-be. It was too much. I started tearing up immediately. "This is going to be an interesting couple of hours," I said. "I promise not to cry too much."

The theme of their meal was an Italian feast, and I made it as far as the focaccia before I broke my promise. By the tiramisu, my tear ducts were dry. I cried so much not because of the food, which was incredibly delicious, but because I was just so proud of my son. His childhood had its own challenges, but he had grown into a lovely young man, he was marrying a wonderful young woman, and he was so very happy, and I was allowing myself to feel it. I don't know if this makes sense, but his happiness filled me with the kind of intense joy I had always wanted and hoped to feel. A couple of weeks later, I flew to Houston to see Wolfie and his band open a new leg of their tour. I try to go to all the opening nights (and maybe a few others, but hey, who's counting?). This one was especially fun because it was at a smaller venue, and during soundcheck the band ran through a bunch of new songs from Wolfie's second album. They were working through the parts since the songs hadn't been released yet. Not only did they sound great, I realized I might like soundcheck as much as the actual live show because then, I like to watch the audience react to the music.

My brother Patrick, his wife, Stacy, Andraia, Wolfie, and I had a group text going, as we do when we're all on the road together, so we can keep track of each other's whereabouts throughout the night as we wander around the venue. Just before the show, I texted, "I'm up in the balcony, on the side of the stage, if you want to come up. Where are you?" I intended it for Stacy, but Wolfie replied instead. "I'm on stage." I'm sure Wolfie heard my laugh as I read his text. He might've looked up at me during the show.

I stayed in that spot to the very end, and I was still there when Wolfie took a final bow with his band and pointed his finger up to his dad, as was his routine at the end of every show. But right before he did that, he looked toward where I stood in the balcony and asked, "Good show, Ma?" I shouted, "Great show, baby." And then I sat down in a chair all by myself and cried knowing that this was dessert, my dessert, and feeling ever so grateful I had figured out how to enjoy it.

Pisang Goreng

(page 292)

DESSERT

"I'm more of a savory girl, but I answer when my sweet tooth calls. It's a great way to celebrate the day."

Blueberry Clafoutis

I don't like attaching the word "healthy" to any food, but one day, while leafing through a magazine, I read that frozen blueberries retain more antioxidants than fresh blueberries, and my first thought was "Clafoutis!" Basically a custard cake, it's a very easy, beautiful, and elegant dessert to serve to company. It's worth every bite. And as far as I'm concerned, it's a great vehicle for all of those antioxidants that are good for me.

3 large eggs, room temperature

½ cup all-purpose flour

2 teaspoons vanilla extract

¼ teaspoon almond extract

⅓ cup granulated sugar

1⅓ cups whole milk, room temperature

1 teaspoon lemon zest

1 tablespoon unsalted butter, room temperature

2 cups frozen blueberries, thawed and drained on paper towels

Powdered sugar, for serving

Preheat the oven to 375°F.

Combine the eggs, flour, vanilla, almond extract, granulated sugar, milk, and lemon zest in a high-powered blender and blend until smooth and light, about 1 minute. Let sit at room temperature for 5 minutes.

Use the butter to coat a 9-inch pie plate. Place the prepared pie plate on a baking sheet.

Arrange the thawed berries on the base of the pie plate. Stir the rested batter, then gently pour it over the berries. Transfer the baking sheet to the oven to bake for 35 to 40 minutes, until the center of the custard is set and the clafoutis is golden brown and puffed.

Let the clafoutis sit for 10 minutes before dusting with powdered sugar, cutting into wedges, and serving. The clafoutis will deflate as it sits.

Carrot Ginger Loaf

There's something about loaf cakes that I love. It might be that they remind me of the old Pepperidge Farm cakes I had when I was a kid. In fact, this is basically my mom's carrot cake recipe with a few more delicious ingredients, but I'm making it in a loaf pan. The orange glaze pumps up the flavor. And the crystalized ginger is because I love it.

For the Carrot Ginger Loaf

Cooking spray

1½ cups all-purpose flour

1 teaspoon baking soda

1 teaspoon baking powder

¼ teaspoon kosher salt

2 teaspoons pumpkin pie spice

½ cup neutral oil, such as vegetable oil, avocado oil, or grapeseed oil

2 large eggs, room temperature

¼ cup whole milk, room temperature

¾ cup packed light brown sugar

2 teaspoons vanilla extract

1 tablespoon fresh grated ginger

1½ cups grated carrot (about 3 medium carrots)

⅓ cup chopped pecans

¼ cup golden raisins

For the Orange Glaze

1 cup powdered sugar

2 teaspoons orange zest

2 tablespoons freshly squeezed orange juice

¼ cup chopped crystalized ginger

Preheat the oven to 350°F. Spray a 9 × 5-inch loaf pan with cooking spray.

To make the cake, whisk together the flour, baking soda, baking powder, salt, and pumpkin pie spice in a large bowl.

In a separate large bowl, whisk together the oil, eggs, milk, brown sugar, vanilla, ginger, and carrot. Add the wet ingredients to the dry ingredients and mix until just combined and no streaks of flour remain. Fold in the pecans and raisins with a silicone spatula.

Pour the batter into the prepared loaf pan and spread it out evenly. Bake for 45 minutes, until a toothpick inserted in the center comes out clean. If the top starts to brown too much, feel free to tent it with foil.

Let the loaf cool in the pan for 10 minutes before turning it out onto a wire rack to cool completely.

To make the glaze, combine the powdered sugar and orange zest in a small bowl. Add the orange juice and stir until the glaze is smooth and pourable.

Cover the top of the cooled loaf with the glaze and then top with the crystalized ginger. Let the glaze set for 15 minutes before slicing.

Chocolate Nuggets

I thought I had made most of my mom's old cookie recipes, but then I found this one tucked in the back of her recipe box. Though I hadn't seen it before, it was in her handwriting, and I could tell by the ingredients that it was from the 1950s or '60s. I whipped up a batch; they were so delicious and chewy I wanted to share them. A good cookie never goes out of style.

8 ounces vanilla wafers

6 ounces semisweet chocolate, chopped

3 tablespoons light corn syrup

1 teaspoon vanilla extract

½ cup evaporated milk

½ cup powdered sugar

2 cups finely chopped walnuts

Place the vanilla wafers in a food processor and pulse until finely crushed. The crumbs should look like sand. You should end up with about 2 cups of wafer crumbs.

Set up a double boiler: Fill a medium pot with an inch or so of hot water. Place the chocolate in a medium heatproof bowl and set it over the pot. Make sure that the base of the bowl is not touching the water. Bring the water to a simmer and keep on low heat. Stir the chocolate until melted.

Remove the bowl from the double boiler and add the corn syrup and vanilla. Stir until evenly combined. Add the evaporated milk in three increments, making sure that the milk is combined with the chocolate mixture before adding more. Next, add the powdered sugar, wafer crumbs, and ½ cup of the walnuts. Mix well to combine. Refrigerate the mixture for 20 minutes.

Line a baking sheet with parchment paper.

Use a 1-tablespoon cookie scoop to scoop portions of the dough. Roll into a ball and then roll in the remaining chopped nuts. Set on the prepared baking sheet. Chill in the fridge for at least an hour before serving.

Chocolate Peanut Butter Dates

I was new to TikTok and trying to figure out what it was all about when I came across a video that inspired these chocolate peanut butter dates. My reaction was OMG! And it's still OMG! Carefully slice the dates open, stuff them with peanut butter, bathe them in chocolate, and then please do your best to let them sit in the fridge. I put down 15 minutes; they're even better if you can hold out for 30 minutes or longer, though I understand if you can't.

10 dates

3 to 4 tablespoons smooth or crunchy peanut butter—your preference! (page 310 or store-bought)

6 ounces bittersweet chocolate, chopped

Flaky sea salt

Line a small baking sheet with parchment paper.

Cut a slit lengthwise in each of the dates and remove the pit. Be sure not to cut all the way through the date; you should be able to open it like a book. Use a butter knife or an offset spatula to smear about 1 teaspoon of the peanut butter inside a date, pressing it into the space where the pit was. Close the date and scrape away any excess peanut butter that oozes out. Place the date on the prepared baking sheet and repeat with the remaining dates and peanut butter.

Transfer the stuffed dates to the freezer for 15 minutes.

Meanwhile, melt the chocolate in a double boiler (see page 291) or in the microwave in 15-second increments until melted.

Remove the dates from the freezer. Working with one at a time, place the date in the melted chocolate and use two forks to turn the date, completely coating it in the chocolate. Lift the date up with the forks, letting any excess chocolate drip back into the bowl. Place the date back on the prepared baking sheet and continue dipping the rest of the dates in the chocolate. Sprinkle with flaky salt.

Refrigerate the chocolate-coated dates until set, at least 15 minutes. Dates can be stored in the fridge for up to 5 days.

Cream Cheese Brownies

If you're going to title a cookbook *Indulge*, you need at least one dessert that looks and tastes like Willy Wonka's mom made it. Here you go! These cream cheese brownies are rich, gooey, chewy, and oh-so-chocolatey good. Cut into bars, squares, or—no, this is not one giant brownie . . . unless it needs to be.

For the Brownie

Cooking spray

4 ounces Baker's German's Sweet Chocolate, chopped

3 tablespoons unsalted butter, room temperature

2 large eggs, room temperature

¾ cup sugar

½ cup all-purpose flour

½ teaspoon baking powder

¼ teaspoon kosher salt

1 teaspoon vanilla extract

¼ teaspoon almond extract

½ cup finely chopped walnuts

For the Cream Cheese Layer

2 tablespoons unsalted butter, room temperature

3 ounces cream cheese

¼ cup sugar

1 large egg, room temperature

1 tablespoon all-purpose flour

1 teaspoon vanilla extract

Preheat the oven to 350°F. Lightly spray an 8 × 8-inch baking dish with cooking spray, then line the pan with parchment paper, allowing 2 to 3 inches of overhang on two of the sides. This will enable you to easily remove the brownies from the baking dish. Spray the parchment paper with cooking spray.

To make the brownie batter, set up a double boiler: Fill a medium pot with an inch or so of hot water. Place the chocolate and butter in a medium heatproof bowl and set it over the pot. Make sure that the base of the bowl is not touching the water. Bring the water to a simmer and keep on low heat. Stir until the chocolate and butter are melted and evenly combined. Remove the bowl from the double boiler and let the chocolate mixture cool to room temperature.

Once the chocolate mixture has cooled, using an electric hand mixer, mix the eggs and sugar in a large bowl until pale yellow and fluffy, about 2 minutes. Add the flour, baking powder, and salt and blend until smooth. Add the cooled chocolate mixture, vanilla, and almond extract and mix until no white spots remain. Use a silicone spatula to fold in the nuts. To make the cream cheese layer, use an electric hand mixer to cream the butter and cream cheese together in a medium bowl until evenly combined, stopping to scrape down the sides of the bowl as necessary. While mixing, gradually add in the sugar and beat until fluffy, 2 to 3 minutes. Add the egg, flour, and vanilla and mix until smooth.

Remove and reserve 1 cup of the brownie batter. Add the remaining brownie batter to the prepared baking dish and spread in an even layer. Top with the cream cheese mixture, gently spreading it into an even layer without disturbing the chocolate layer beneath. Dollop the reserved brownie mixture on top of the cream cheese and use a spatula to marble it. Bake for 35 to 40 minutes, until a toothpick inserted in the center comes out mostly clean. Let cool before cutting into bars or squares.

Espresso Affogato

Affogato is essentially a scoop of vanilla gelato swimming in a shot or two of espresso. You can use decaf espresso without sacrificing any flavor or, more importantly, any precious sleep.

1 lemon

2 scoops No-Churn Buttermilk Vanilla Ice Cream (page 296 or store-bought vanilla)

2 shots espresso

Use a vegetable peeler to remove a long strip of peel from the lemon. Set aside.

Scoop the ice cream into a martini glass. Pour the espresso over the ice cream. Squeeze the lemon peel over the glass to release the essential oils and aromas. Add the peel to the glass as garnish. Enjoy immediately.

Pisang Goreng

PHOTO ON PAGE 280

Mrs. Van Halen taught me how to make this dessert. I made it for Wolfie a few years ago and told him that his grandma used to make it for his dad and me. "And you're only making it for me now?" he said. I apologized. It's crazy delicious.

1 cup all-purpose flour

½ cup club soda

½ cup milk

2 tablespoons powdered sugar, plus more for serving

1 teaspoon cornstarch

1 teaspoon vanilla extract

¼ teaspoon kosher salt

2 ripe bananas, cut into 1-inch diagonal slices

Vegetable oil, for frying

Whisk together the flour, club soda, milk, powdered sugar, cornstarch, vanilla, and salt in a medium bowl until well combined and smooth. Add the sliced bananas and stir to coat completely. Cover the bowl with plastic wrap and refrigerate while the oil heats.

Add about 1 inch of oil to a Dutch oven or heavy-bottomed skillet. Heat the oil to 350°F over medium to high heat. Place a wire rack inside a baking sheet.

Once the oil is hot, remove the bananas from the fridge. Working with a few slices at a time, remove the bananas from the batter, letting any excess drip back into the bowl. Transfer to the hot oil and fry until golden brown, 1 to 2 minutes per side. Use a slotted spoon to transfer the bananas to the wire rack. Repeat with the remaining banana slices. Dust with powdered sugar and serve.

Lemon Lime White Chocolate Chip Cookies

Whenever I made these on *Valerie's Home Cooking,* I had to make three or four extra batches for everyone on the crew. They are that delicious. At home, I still make extra and divvy up the dough into small batches, throw it into baggies, and freeze them until needed. They cook up as fresh as ever. Just ask Wolfie's band. I took some to rehearsal, and they devoured them. A year later, they still talk about "those incredible cookies."

2¼ cups all-purpose flour

1 teaspoon baking soda

¼ teaspoon kosher salt

2 sticks (1 cup) unsalted butter, room temperature

¾ cup packed light brown sugar

¾ cup granulated sugar

1 large egg, room temperature

2 tablespoons lemon zest (from 2 lemons)

2 tablespoons lime zest (from 3 limes)

1 tablespoon vanilla extract

2 cups white chocolate chips

Preheat the oven to 375°F. Line two baking sheets with parchment paper.

Whisk together the flour, baking soda, and salt in a medium bowl.

Combine the butter and sugars in the bowl of a stand mixer fitted with the paddle attachment. Mix on high speed until lighter in color and fluffy, 1 to 2 minutes, stopping to scrape down the bowl as needed. Add the egg and beat until incorporated. Add the lemon zest, lime zest, and vanilla and beat until evenly combined. Add the dry ingredients to the butter-sugar mixture and mix until just incorporated. Remove the bowl from the stand mixer and fold the chocolate chips in with a silicone spatula.

Use a 1-tablespoon cookie scoop to scoop the dough onto the prepared baking sheets, placing them 2 inches apart. Each tray should hold 12 to 16 cookies. Bake for 8 to 10 minutes, until the edges are golden brown and the centers are still soft.

Allow the cookies to cool on the baking sheets for 5 minutes, then transfer them to a wire rack to cool completely. Repeat with the remaining dough.

Cook's Note	The cookie dough can be wrapped in plastic wrap, placed in a zip-top bag, and frozen for up to 1 month.

No-Churn Buttermilk Vanilla Ice Cream

This is a delicious no-churn vanilla ice cream. You can use it in a sundae, a shake, on top of a pie or tart, or all by itself. The rich, beautiful vanilla flavor is something to savor. The buttermilk adds extra tang, making it taste even better.

One 14-ounce can sweetened condensed milk

2 teaspoons vanilla extract

⅛ teaspoon kosher salt

1¼ cups heavy cream

¾ cup buttermilk

Place a 9 × 5-inch loaf pan in the freezer for 15 minutes to chill.

Whisk together the condensed milk, vanilla, and salt in a large bowl.

Using an electric hand mixer on high, whip the cream and buttermilk in a separate large bowl until stiff peaks form, about 5 minutes. Working in batches, delicately fold the whipped cream with a silicone spatula into the sweetened condensed milk mixture, making sure it's fully incorporated before adding another batch.

Remove the loaf pan from the freezer. Pour the mixture into the cold pan. Loosely cover with plastic wrap and return to the freezer. Freeze until solid, 6 to 8 hours or overnight. Scoop into bowls and serve.

No-Churn Chocolate Peanut Butter Ice Cream

I first learned about the genius of no-churn ice cream on *Kids Baking Championship*, and so of course the first time I made it I wanted to go back to being that kid ordering her favorite sundae at Farrell's Ice Cream Parlor. Here's a little taste of my childhood just for you.

For the Ice Cream Base

2 cups heavy cream, chilled

1 teaspoon vanilla extract

One 14-ounce can sweetened condensed milk

For the Chocolate Sauce

¼ cup cocoa powder

½ cup sugar

Kosher salt

½ teaspoon vanilla extract

For the Peanut Butter Sauce

½ cup crunchy or creamy peanut butter (page 310 or store-bought)

Topping

½ cup roasted, salted peanuts, roughly chopped

In the bowl of a stand mixer fitted with the whisk attachment, combine the cream and vanilla and whip on high speed until stiff peaks form, about 5 minutes. While the cream is whipping, pour the condensed milk into a large bowl.

With a silicone spatula, gently fold half the whipped cream into the condensed milk. Add the remaining whipped cream and fold in until combined. Transfer the mixture to a 9 × 5-inch loaf pan or other freezer-safe container. Cover with plastic wrap, placing it directly on the surface of the mixture. Freeze until partially frozen but still scoopable, 2 to 3 hours.

Meanwhile, to make the chocolate sauce, whisk together the cocoa powder, sugar, and a pinch of salt in a small saucepan until no lumps remain. Add ¼ cup of water and whisk again to incorporate. Bring the mixture to a boil over medium-high heat. Remove from the heat, whisk in the vanilla, and set aside to cool.

To make the peanut butter sauce, heat the peanut butter in a separate small saucepan over medium heat until it's more easily spreadable. Remove from the heat and let cool slightly.

Remove the ice cream base from the freezer. Scoop out half into a bowl. Pour half of the chocolate sauce over the base and swirl with a knife. Add half of the peanut butter sauce and swirl. Sprinkle half of the peanuts over the sauces. Place the removed ice cream base back into the loaf pan. Smooth the top and add the remaining chocolate sauce and peanut sauce and swirl. Top with the remaining peanuts. Cover with plastic wrap and return to the freezer to set up for 2 to 3 hours.

Scoop into bowls and serve.

PB&J Cups

I went through a stage when I was fixated on Reese's Peanut Butter Cups. Who hasn't? And who doesn't love a good PB&J? I combined the two. I highly recommend using bittersweet chocolate, which will balance the jam and peanut butter. Milk chocolate will be too sweet. This is a "wow" dessert; whether serving to family or friends, I swear you will get a round of applause.

12 ounces bittersweet
　chocolate chips
¾ cup smooth peanut butter
½ cup confectioners' sugar
Cooking spray
6 tablespoons strawberry jelly
Flaky sea salt, for garnish
　(optional)

Line 8 cups of a 12-cup muffin tin with cupcake liners.

Set up a double boiler: Fill a medium pot with an inch or so of hot water. Place the chocolate in a medium heatproof bowl and set it over the pot. Make sure that the base of the bowl is not touching the water. Bring the water to a simmer and keep on medium heat. Stir the chocolate until melted. Remove from the heat.

Using an electric hand mixer, mix the peanut butter and confectioners' sugar in a medium bowl until well combined. Set the peanut butter mixture aside.

Spoon 1 tablespoon of melted chocolate into each cupcake liner. Use a 1-tablespoon cookie scoop to portion the peanut butter mixture into your hand. If the mixture is too sticky, lightly spray your hands with cooking spray. Slightly flatten the peanut butter, but make sure to keep it smaller than the base of the muffin cup so that the chocolate can encase it. Place the peanut butter on top of the chocolate, pressing lightly to let the chocolate come slightly up the sides of the peanut butter. Repeat with the remaining muffin cups.

Next, use a ½-tablespoon cookie scoop to scoop a portion of jelly on top of the peanut butter. To finish the cups, top the peanut butter and jelly with an additional 1 tablespoon of melted chocolate. Use a spoon to spread the chocolate to completely cover the peanut butter and jelly. Sprinkle each cup with flaky salt, if desired. Transfer the muffin tin to the fridge until completely set, about 30 minutes.

The PB&J cups can be stored in an airtight container in the fridge for up to 5 days or the freezer for up to 1 month.

Pineapple Upside-Down Cake

Inspired by my mom yet again, I made a pineapple upside-down cake on *Valerie's Home Cooking,* and it was, not to boast, a picture I wanted everyone to see. I felt like a kid again. *I did that.* The cake was sensational—wonderfully dense, infused with the sweetness of the pineapple, and topped with Italian cherries soaked in brandy. You don't make this every day, so go ahead, indulge.

For the Topping

½ stick (4 tablespoons) unsalted butter, melted

½ cup packed light brown sugar

One 20-ounce can pineapple rings, drained and patted dry (10 rings)

19 brandy-soaked cherries, drained

For the Cake

1½ cups cake flour

2 teaspoons baking powder

½ teaspoon kosher salt

¼ teaspoon ground cinnamon

1 stick (8 tablespoons) unsalted butter, room temperature

¾ cup packed light brown sugar

2 large eggs, room temperature

1 tablespoon vanilla extract

1 tablespoon orange zest

1 cup sour cream

Preheat the oven to 350°F. Line a baking sheet with foil.

To make the topping, pour the melted butter into a 9-inch pie plate. Use a pastry brush to brush the sides of the pie plate with the butter. Sprinkle with the brown sugar. Use clean hands to cover the base and sides of the pie plate with the butter-sugar mixture. Arrange 7 pineapple rings on the base of the pie plate. Cut the remaining 3 rings in half and place them in the openings on the sides of the pie plate. Place a cherry in the center of each pineapple ring and in the empty spaces among the pineapple rings. Place the pie plate in the fridge while you make the batter.

To make the cake, combine the flour, baking powder, salt, and cinnamon in a bowl and whisk until evenly combined and any lumps of flour are broken up. Set aside.

Place the butter and brown sugar in the bowl of a stand mixer fitted with the paddle attachment and mix on medium-high speed until light and fluffy, about 2 minutes. Add the eggs, one at a time, waiting until the first egg is fully incorporated before adding the other. Add the vanilla and orange zest and mix until combined.

Alternate adding the flour mixture and the sour cream to the mixer, starting and ending with the flour mixture. Mix until just combined. Spoon the batter into the chilled pie plate. Place the pie plate on the prepared baking sheet and transfer to the oven to bake for 45 to 50 minutes, until the juices are bubbling and a toothpick inserted in the center of the cake comes out clean.

Transfer to a wire rack to cool for 15 minutes. Place a plate over the top of the cake and carefully flip the cake over, inverting it onto the plate. Let cool for an additional 10 to 15 minutes before serving.

Strawberry Pretzel Salad

Wolfie, his wife, and I were sitting around one night, talking about our favorite foods, and I asked Andraia to name her favorite dessert. She said, "Strawberry pretzel salad." I'd never heard of it. None of those words even went together. And yet here it is—basically Jell-O with fresh strawberries, sweetened cream cheese, and a crushed pretzel pie-like crust, which puts it over the top. I mean . . . it's insanely good! But I still don't understand why it's called a salad.

For the Crust

Cooking spray

2½ cups mini pretzel twists

5 tablespoons unsalted
   butter, melted

1 tablespoon sugar

For the Cream Cheese Layer

5 ounces cream cheese, room
   temperature

⅓ cup sugar

1 teaspoon vanilla extract

5 ounces Cool Whip, thawed

For the Strawberry Topping

One 3-ounce package
   strawberry Jell-O

1 cup boiling water

2 cups sliced strawberries

Preheat the oven to 350°F. Lightly spray an 8 × 8-inch baking dish with cooking spray, then line the pan with parchment paper, allowing 2 to 3 inches of overhang on two of the sides. This will enable you to easily remove the dessert from the baking dish when it's set. Lightly spray the parchment paper with cooking spray.

To make the crust, place the pretzels in a food processor and pulse until the pretzels are broken up and no pieces are larger than a pea. This should yield about 1 cup of crushed pretzels.

Stir together the crushed pretzels, melted butter, and sugar in a large bowl. The mixture should look like a slightly chunky wet sand. Transfer the mixture to the prepared baking dish and use clean hands or the base of a measuring cup to press it into a compact, even layer. Bake for 15 minutes, until lightly golden and set. Let cool completely on a wire rack before continuing with the next steps.

To make the cream cheese layer, using an electric hand mixer, beat the cream cheese, sugar, and vanilla in a large bowl until fully incorporated and light and fluffy, about 2 minutes, stopping to scrape down the sides of the bowl as necessary. Fold in the Cool Whip until evenly combined. Dollop the mixture over the cooled crust and use an offset spatula to spread it into an even layer, completely covering the crust. Cover with plastic wrap and refrigerate until set, 1 hour.

To make the strawberry topping, mix together the strawberry Jell-O and boiling water in a large bowl or heatproof measuring cup. Let cool to room temperature.

Layer the sliced strawberries on top of the cream cheese mixture. Gently pour the cooled gelatin mixture over the strawberries. Cover and refrigerate until the Jell-O is completely set, 2 to 3 hours.

Use an offset spatula to loosen the Jell-O from the edges of the baking dish, then use the parchment paper overhang to help you lift the dessert out of the baking dish and onto a cutting board. Cut into bars or squares.

JAMS, SPREADS & HONEYS

"When I spread a good jam or honey, I think of my childhood and smile. I get all that in a jar!"

Citrus Curd
(page 309)

Hot Honey
(page 308)

Homemade
Peanut Butter
(page 310)

Turmeric
Ginger Honey
(page 311)

Strawberry
Rhubarb
Jam
(page 311)

Bacon Jam
(page 308)

Bacon Jam

PHOTO ON PAGE 307

Who else loves bacon and sweet homemade jam? Count me in on both. Bacon jam originated in Europe before becoming popular online—and in my kitchen. It's quick and easy to make, and the best part is the savory-sweet aroma that fills your kitchen. Enjoy it with soft scrambled eggs, use it as a sandwich spread, or add it to a grilled cheese or hamburger for extra flavor.

1 pound thick-cut bacon, cut into ½-inch pieces

2 sweet onions (such as Vidalia or Walla Walla), chopped

2 tablespoons light brown sugar

¼ teaspoon cayenne pepper

3 garlic cloves, grated

¼ cup balsamic vinegar

Toast, for serving

Chopped chives, for garnish

Place the bacon in a skillet and cook over medium heat until it's just starting to brown slightly and render its fat, 3 to 4 minutes. Add the onions and stir to combine. Cook, stirring occasionally, until the onions are soft and almost melting into the bacon fat, 30 to 40 minutes. If the pan starts to look dry or the mixture is browning too much, add a splash of water.

Stir in the brown sugar, cayenne, and garlic, then add the balsamic vinegar. Cook until the sugar dissolves and the mixture is thick, about 5 minutes. Remove from the heat.

Cool slightly and transfer the mixture to a food processor and pulse until the bacon is chopped slightly finer, 5 to 6 pulses.

To serve, spread on toast and garnish with chives.

Hot Honey

PHOTO ON PAGE 307

Hot honey has been a thing in restaurants and grocery stores for nearly two decades. After noticing people snapping it up at my local farmers' market, I decided to make my own. I love bold, contrasting flavors; the sweet-and-spicy combo suits me. I use locally sourced honey for its supposed allergy benefits and enjoy adding a touch of heat to anything I would typically sweeten with honey.

1 cup honey

2 teaspoons red pepper flakes

2 teaspoons apple cider vinegar

Combine the honey and pepper flakes in a small saucepan. Bring the mixture to a simmer over medium heat, then remove from the heat and stir in the vinegar. Let cool to room temperature. Once it's cooled, strain it into an airtight container and store at room temperature for up to 3 months.

Citrus Curd

PHOTO ON PAGE 307

There are many kinds of curd, but lemon curd is my favorite. Try it with limes, oranges, and grapefruit. I vary according to whichever is most abundant on the trees in my yard. This recipe is especially easy because it's made entirely in the microwave. It pairs perfectly with fresh berries or as a topping on morning pancakes. For a quick treat, I have a spoonful straight up and enjoy that burst of creamy citrus on my tongue. Yum.

1 stick (8 tablespoons) unsalted butter

1 cup sugar

¼ teaspoon kosher salt

3 large eggs plus 1 large egg yolk

¼ cup lemon zest (or lime zest), from 3 to 4 lemons (or 5 to 6 limes)

1 cup freshly squeezed lemon juice (or lime juice), from 5 to 7 lemons (or 8 limes)

Melt the butter in a medium microwave-safe bowl in 30-second intervals. Add the sugar and salt and whisk to combine. Add the eggs and egg yolk and whisk again. Finally, add the citrus zest and juice and whisk well to combine. Microwave for 1 minute. Carefully remove the bowl and whisk. Continue to microwave in 1-minute intervals, whisking after each minute, until the mixture is thick. This will take between 5 and 10 minutes, depending on the microwave. The mixture will get thin before it gets thick. Use caution removing the bowl from the microwave, as it can get fairly hot.

Cover the curd with plastic wrap and cool to room temperature before transferring to an airtight container. Store in the fridge for up to 2 weeks.

Homemade Peanut Butter

A good peanut butter and jelly sandwich is something we enjoy as children but forget to treat ourselves to as adults. All the ingredients you need for this classic sandwich are in this book—bread, Strawberry Rhubarb Jam (page 311), and now peanut butter. Or go for another classic: a peanut butter, banana, and honey sandwich. Peanut butter also goes well straight off the spoon. I prefer mine chunky, but you can adjust it to your liking.

PHOTO ON PAGE 307

3 cups unsalted dry-roasted peanuts

1 tablespoon honey

¼ teaspoon kosher salt

Place the peanuts in a food processor and process for 3 minutes. The peanuts will first break down and look like wet sand, then the mixture will form into a ball and eventually thin out to a spreadable, creamy consistency. After 3 minutes, add the honey and salt, then process for an additional 2 minutes until smooth.

Transfer the peanut butter to an airtight container and store at room temperature for up to 2 weeks or in the fridge for up to 1 month.

Cook's Note

If you prefer a chunky peanut butter, stir in about ¼ cup of finely chopped peanuts after processing.

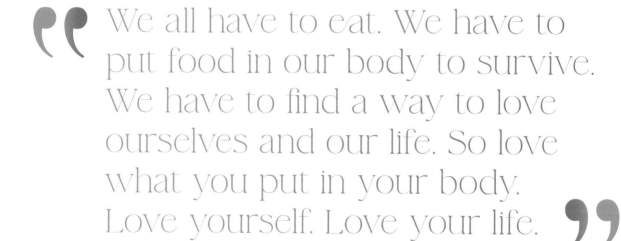

"We all have to eat. We have to put food in our body to survive. We have to find a way to love ourselves and our life. So love what you put in your body. Love yourself. Love your life."

Strawberry Rhubarb Jam

PHOTO ON PAGE 307

My mom made a strawberry rhubarb pie whenever rhubarb was in season, and so I am indulging that memory with this recipe. The funny thing is, as a kid, I thought strawberry and rhubarb together was the weirdest combination of tastes, yet it got more delicious with each bite I took. Whether on toast, in little pastry cups, or between layers of a cake, the taste always delights me.

1 pound strawberries, hulled and roughly chopped

1 pound rhubarb, roughly chopped

1 cup sugar

2 tablespoons freshly squeezed lemon juice

2 tablespoons freshly squeezed orange juice

¼ teaspoon kosher salt

Combine the strawberries, rhubarb, sugar, lemon and orange juice, and salt in a medium saucepan or Dutch oven. Cook over medium-low heat until the sugar is dissolved, about 4 minutes. Increase the heat to medium-high and bring the mixture to a boil. Boil for 15 minutes, stirring and mashing the fruit occasionally.

Remove from the heat and let cool. The mixture will thicken as it cools. Transfer to an airtight container and refrigerate for up to 1 month.

Use in peanut butter and jelly sandwiches, yogurt parfaits, or to top ice cream; mix with yogurt and use as a fruit dip; or just spread on buttered toast.

Turmeric Ginger Honey

PHOTO ON PAGE 307

Turmeric is one of those spices that has been around forever, but it has come into vogue for supposedly being an anti-inflammatory and antioxidant, and having numerous other health benefits. I started adding it to my ginger honey and have never stopped. It's good in tea, drizzled on cottage cheese, and added to a smoothie. I will let researchers decide whether it turns a hot toddy into a healthy drink, but it can't hurt.

1 cup honey

1 teaspoon ground turmeric

1 teaspoon ground ginger

1 teaspoon ground cinnamon

¼ teaspoon freshly ground black pepper

½ teaspoon vanilla extract

½ teaspoon lemon zest

Stir together the honey, turmeric, ginger, cinnamon, pepper, vanilla, and lemon zest in a small bowl until well combined. Transfer to a jar and store at room temperature for up to 3 months.

CONDIMENTS, DRESSINGS & SAUCES

"I'm a condiment girl. I have a whole shelf in my refrigerator and I love trying new flavors. It's so easy and fun when you make your own."

I know many of these sauces, condiments, and dressings can be easily purchased in the store, and some might seem intimidating to make, but trust me, they can be re-created from scratch in your kitchen with extra-fresh flavors and no preservatives. You'll love the convenience of having them on hand, too. I pretty much always keep Lemon Herb Vinaigrette (page 325) in my fridge. I use Easy Garlic Chili Crisp (page 330) on sautéed greens, bread, and more. Ketjab is a spicy Indonesian sauce I learned from Mrs. Van Halen and often use in place of soy sauce. And fresh pesto (pages 336–337)? Green Goddess Dressing (page 324)? Homemade Mayo (below)? Come on! These are all so versatile, and you'll see I refer to a lot of them throughout the book. I encourage you to also try them with any dish or recipe that you already love.

Homemade Mayo, Three Ways

Prep time: 5 minutes

Makes about 1¼ cups

Classic Mayo

1 large egg, room temperature

1 tablespoon freshly squeezed lemon juice

1 teaspoon Dijon mustard

¾ teaspoon kosher salt

1 cup neutral oil, such as avocado oil or grapeseed oil

Combine the egg, lemon juice, mustard, salt, and oil in a tall container that just fits an immersion blender. Place the immersion blender in the container, being sure that the blade reaches the egg yolk. Turn the blender on and hold still until the mixture at the bottom starts to thicken and look like mayonnaise. Then, slowly pull the blender up, while still blending, to emulsify the rest of the mixture.

Store in an airtight container in the fridge for up to 1 week.

Roasted Garlic Mayo

For the Roasted Garlic

1 bulb garlic

Extra virgin olive oil

Kosher salt

For the Mayo

1 large egg, room temperature

1 tablespoon freshly squeezed
lemon juice

1 teaspoon Dijon mustard

¾ teaspoon kosher salt

1 cup neutral oil, such
as avocado oil or
grapeseed oil

To roast the garlic, preheat the oven to 400°F. Cut the top
¼ inch off the garlic bulb, exposing the cloves. Place cut side
up on a piece of foil and drizzle with olive oil and a pinch of salt.
Wrap in the foil and roast for 40 to 50 minutes, until the cloves
are tender. Let cool completely.

Once the garlic has cooled, remove the cloves from the skin and
set aside.

To make the mayo, combine the egg, lemon juice, mustard, salt,
and oil in a tall container that just fits an immersion blender.
Place the immersion blender in the container, being sure that
the blade reaches the egg yolk. Turn the blender on and hold
still until the mixture at the bottom starts to thicken and look like
mayonnaise. Then, slowly pull the blender up, while still blending,
to emulsify the rest of the mixture. Add the garlic and blend until
evenly combined.

Store in an airtight container in the fridge for up to 1 week.

Herb Mayo

1 large egg, room temperature

1 tablespoon freshly squeezed
lemon juice

1 teaspoon Dijon mustard

¾ teaspoon kosher salt

1 cup neutral oil, such
as avocado oil or
grapeseed oil

1 tablespoon tarragon leaves

¼ cup loosely packed
basil leaves

Combine the egg, lemon juice, mustard, salt, and oil in
a tall container that just fits an immersion blender. Place the
immersion blender in the container, being sure that the blade
reaches the egg yolk. Turn the blender on and hold still until the
mixture at the bottom starts to thicken and look like mayonnaise.
Then, slowly pull the blender up, while still blending, to emulsify
the rest of the mixture. Add the herbs and blend until green and
evenly combined.

Store in an airtight container in the fridge for up to 1 week.

Homemade
BBQ Sauce
(page 319)

Sambal Oelek
(page 328)

Easy Garlic
Chili Crisp
(page 330)

Roasted
Garlic Mayo
(page 315)

Tapenade
(page 334)

Herb Mayo
(page 315)

Ketjap
(page 329)

Dijon Mustard
(page 318)

Fresno Chile
Hot Sauce
(page 329)

Classic Mayo
(page 314)

Sugar-Free Ketchup

One 12-ounce can tomato paste

½ cup apple cider vinegar

½ teaspoon garlic powder

½ teaspoon onion powder

3 tablespoons brown sugar substitute

1½ teaspoons kosher salt

Whisk together the tomato paste, ½ cup of water, the vinegar, garlic powder, onion powder, brown sugar substitute, and salt in a medium pot. Cook over medium-low heat until the sauce begins to bubble, then cover, reduce the heat to low, and simmer for 10 minutes.

Remove from the heat and let the ketchup cool completely. Store in an airtight container in the fridge for up to 2 months.

Dijon Mustard

1 tablespoon brown mustard seeds

6 tablespoons yellow mustard seeds

⅓ cup distilled white vinegar

3 tablespoons dry white wine

1 tablespoon minced shallot

⅓ cup apple cider vinegar

½ teaspoon garlic powder

1 tablespoon sugar, plus more as needed

½ teaspoon kosher salt

¼ teaspoon freshly ground black pepper

2 tablespoons extra virgin olive oil

Combine the mustard seeds, white vinegar, and 2 tablespoons of the wine in an airtight container. Cover and refrigerate for 24 hours.

After the resting time, drain any remaining liquid. Transfer the mustard seeds, remaining 1 tablespoon wine, shallot, apple cider vinegar, garlic powder, sugar, salt, and pepper to a high-powered blender. Blend on low and slowly increase to medium and high until the mixture comes together and reaches your desired consistency, 2 to 3 minutes. With the machine running, stream in the olive oil. Taste for seasoning and add more sugar if the mustard is too bitter.

Store in an airtight container in the fridge for at least 24 hours before serving. The mustard will last in the fridge for up to 1 month.

Homemade BBQ Sauce

1 cup ketchup

¼ cup apple cider vinegar

3 tablespoons light
   brown sugar

1 teaspoon
   Worcestershire sauce

½ teaspoon garlic powder

½ teaspoon onion powder

½ teaspoon smoked paprika

½ teaspoon liquid smoke

Combine the ketchup, vinegar, brown sugar, Worcestershire sauce, garlic powder, onion powder, smoked paprika, and liquid smoke in a small saucepan. Heat over medium-high heat, stirring occasionally, until simmering, 2 to 3 minutes. Remove from the heat. Use immediately or store in an airtight container in the fridge for up to 2 weeks.

Prep time: 10 minutes
(plus cooling time) | Cook time: 1 hour 5 minutes | Makes 1½ cups

Garlic Confit

1½ cups garlic cloves, root
   ends trimmed

2 cups extra virgin olive oil

Add the garlic to a small saucepan and cover with the olive oil. Heat over medium until the garlic just starts to gently bubble.

Turn the heat down to the lowest setting possible and cook, maintaining a very gentle bubble, for about 1 hour, until the garlic is lightly golden and buttery soft.

Turn off the heat and let the mixture cool completely. Transfer the garlic and olive oil to an airtight container. The garlic can be kept refrigerated for up to 1 month.

The garlic confit can be spread on toast or crackers, used in pasta sauces or as a pizza topping. It can be added to mashed potatoes or even in guacamole!

Classic Ranch Dressing

½ cup mayonnaise

½ cup sour cream

1 tablespoon apple
  cider vinegar

½ teaspoon onion powder

½ teaspoon dried dill

½ teaspoon dried parsley

½ teaspoon dried chives

1 teaspoon garlic powder

Kosher salt and freshly
  ground black pepper

Combine the mayo, sour cream, vinegar, onion powder, dill, parsley, chives, garlic powder, ½ teaspoon salt, and ¼ teaspoon pepper in a blender. Blend on medium-high until the dressing is smooth and creamy, about 1 minute. Season to taste with salt and pepper. Store in an airtight container in the fridge for up to 1 week.

Jalapeño Ranch Dressing

½ cup mayonnaise

½ cup sour cream

1 tablespoon freshly squeezed
  lime juice

¼ cup cilantro leaves

⅓ cup pickled jalapeños,
  thoroughly dried

½ teaspoon onion powder

½ teaspoon dried dill

½ teaspoon dried parsley

½ teaspoon dried chives

1 teaspoon garlic powder

Kosher salt and freshly
  ground black pepper

Combine the mayo, sour cream, lime juice, cilantro, pickled jalapeños, onion powder, dill, parsley, chives, garlic powder, ½ teaspoon salt, and ¼ teaspoon pepper in a food processor. Pulse until everything is evenly combined and mostly smooth. Season to taste with salt and pepper. Store in an airtight container in the fridge for up to 1 week.

Creamy Italian Dressing

⅓ cup mayonnaise

2 tablespoons red
wine vinegar

2 tablespoons extra virgin
olive oil

1 garlic clove, grated

½ teaspoon dried oregano

½ teaspoon dried basil

½ teaspoon dried parsley

1 tablespoon freshly grated
Parmesan

Kosher salt and freshly
ground black pepper

Whisk together the mayo, vinegar, olive oil, garlic, oregano, basil, parsley, Parmesan, ½ teaspoon salt, and ¼ teaspoon pepper in a bowl. Add 1 tablespoon of water to slightly thin the dressing. Season to taste with salt and pepper. Store in an airtight container in the fridge for up to 5 days.

Blue Cheese Dressing

⅔ cup sour cream

½ cup mayonnaise

2 tablespoons freshly
squeezed lemon juice

1 teaspoon Dijon mustard

1 teaspoon honey

1 teaspoon
Worcestershire sauce

1 garlic clove, smashed

Kosher salt and freshly
ground black pepper

¾ cup crumbled blue cheese
(about 5 ounces)

2 tablespoons finely
chopped chives

Combine the sour cream, mayo, lemon juice, mustard, honey, Worcestershire sauce, garlic, ½ teaspoon salt, ¼ teaspoon pepper, and ¼ cup of the blue cheese in a food processor and process until smooth. Transfer the mixture to a small bowl and stir in the remaining ½ cup blue cheese and the chives. Season to taste with salt and pepper. Store in an airtight container in the fridge for up to 1 week.

Green
Goddess
Dressing
(page 324)

Classic Ranch
Dressing (page 320)

Jalapeño
Ranch
Dressing
(page 320)

Ginger
Miso
Dressing
(page 326)

Lemon Herb
Vinaigrette
(page 325)

Dill Pickle
Vinaigrette
(page 327)

Shallot
Dressing
(page 326)

Red Wine
Vinaigrette
(page 325)

Blue Cheese
Dressing
(page 321)

Lemon
Caesar
Dressing
(page 324)

Creamy Italian
Dressing
(page 321)

Honey
Mustard
Dressing
(page 327)

Calabrian Chili
Vinaigrette
(page 328)

Green Goddess Dressing

¾ cup fat-free Greek yogurt

¼ cup mayonnaise

¼ cup freshly squeezed lemon
  juice (from 2 lemons)

1 garlic clove, smashed

1 cup parsley leaves

3 tablespoons tarragon leaves

¼ cup chopped chives

1 green onion, white
  and light green parts,
  roughly chopped

½ teaspoon kosher salt

¼ teaspoon freshly ground
  black pepper

Combine the yogurt, mayo, lemon juice, garlic, parsley, tarragon, chives, green onion, salt, and pepper in a blender. Start blending on low speed, gradually increasing the speed to medium-high, until bright green and smooth, about 20 seconds. Store in an airtight container in the fridge for up to 5 days.

Lemon Caesar Dressing

3 garlic cloves, grated

1½ teaspoons anchovy
  paste (or 3 anchovy fillets,
  finely minced)

1 tablespoon chopped capers

2 teaspoons Dijon mustard

⅓ cup freshly squeezed lemon
  juice (from 2 to 3 lemons)

1 tablespoon
  Worcestershire sauce

½ cup extra virgin olive oil

Kosher salt and freshly
  ground black pepper

⅓ cup freshly grated
  Parmesan (about
  1½ ounces)

Combine the garlic, anchovy paste, capers, mustard, lemon juice, Worcestershire, olive oil, ½ teaspoon salt, and ¼ teaspoon pepper in a blender or a wide-mouth jar that fits an immersion blender. Blend until combined and mostly smooth. Add the Parmesan and blend until just combined. Season to taste with salt and pepper. Store in an airtight container in the fridge for 3 to 5 days.

Lemon Herb Vinaigrette

⅓ cup extra virgin olive oil

1 teaspoon lemon zest

¼ cup freshly squeezed lemon juice (from 2 lemons)

2 tablespoons rice vinegar

2 teaspoons Dijon mustard

2 tablespoons chopped parsley

2 tablespoons chopped chives

1 teaspoon chopped dill

1 garlic clove, grated

½ teaspoon kosher salt

¼ teaspoon freshly ground black pepper

Combine the olive oil, lemon zest and juice, vinegar, mustard, parsley, chives, dill, garlic, salt, and pepper in a medium bowl and whisk to combine. Store in an airtight container in the fridge for up to 5 days.

If you have a dressing carafe or mason jar, add all the ingredients, shake it up to combine, and store the dressing in that!

Red Wine Vinaigrette

½ cup red wine vinegar

⅓ cup extra virgin olive oil

1 tablespoon minced shallot

1 teaspoon honey

½ teaspoon Dijon mustard

¼ teaspoon kosher salt

Red pepper flakes

Combine the vinegar, olive oil, shallot, honey, mustard, salt, and a pinch of pepper flakes in a jar with a lid. Cover and shake until emulsified. Store in the fridge for up to 1 week.

Shallot Dressing

1 large shallot

1 garlic clove

1 tablespoon Dijon mustard

⅓ cup extra virgin olive oil

⅓ cup apple cider vinegar

1 teaspoon dried chives

1 teaspoon dried parsley

½ teaspoon kosher salt

¼ teaspoon freshly ground black pepper

Combine the shallot, garlic, mustard, olive oil, vinegar, chives, parsley, salt, and pepper in a blender. Blend until smooth. Store in an airtight container in the fridge for up to 5 days.

Ginger Miso Dressing

3 tablespoons yellow miso paste

3 tablespoons grated ginger

2 tablespoons freshly squeezed lime juice

3 tablespoons low-sodium soy sauce

3 tablespoons canola oil

3 tablespoons rice vinegar

1 tablespoon toasted sesame oil

1 tablespoon toasted sesame seeds

Combine the miso paste, ginger, lime juice, soy sauce, canola oil, vinegar, sesame oil, and sesame seeds in a jar with a lid. Cover and shake until emulsified. Store in an airtight container in the fridge for up to 1 week.

Honey Mustard Dressing

⅓ cup extra virgin olive oil

¼ cup white wine vinegar

1 tablespoon finely
   minced shallot

2 tablespoons honey mustard

Kosher salt and freshly
   ground black pepper

Combine the olive oil, vinegar, shallot, honey mustard,
¼ teaspoon salt, and a pinch of pepper in a jar with a lid. Cover
and shake vigorously to emulsify. Season to taste with salt and
pepper. Store in the fridge for up to 1 week.

Dill Pickle Vinaigrette

¼ cup dill pickle juice

⅓ cup extra virgin olive oil

1 small garlic clove, grated

1 heaping tablespoon roughly
   chopped dill

2 teaspoons Dijon mustard

1 tablespoon freshly squeezed
   lemon juice

½ teaspoon kosher salt

¼ teaspoon freshly ground
   black pepper

Whisk together the dill pickle juice, olive oil, garlic, dill, mustard,
lemon juice, salt, and pepper in a small bowl. Store in an airtight
container in the fridge for up to 7 days.

Calabrian Chili Vinaigrette

½ cup extra virgin olive oil

⅓ cup red wine vinegar

1 teaspoon Dijon mustard

2 teaspoons Calabrian
  chili paste

1 garlic clove, grated

¼ cup freshly grated
  Parmesan (about 1 ounce)

¾ teaspoon dried oregano

¾ teaspoon kosher salt

Combine the olive oil, vinegar, mustard, chili paste, garlic, Parmesan, oregano, and salt in a jar with a lid. Cover and shake to emulsify. Store in the fridge for up to 5 days.

Sambal Oelek

This spicy Indonesian sauce is not for the faint of heart. To tone down the heat, you can use a mixture of Fresno and Thai chiles and remove the seeds. Mrs. Van Halen used it to braise chicken and give her soups and noodles a blast of intense flavor, which I can vouch for.

1 pound red Thai chiles,
  stemmed*

3 garlic cloves, smashed

1 teaspoon kosher salt

1 teaspoon sugar

3 tablespoons rice vinegar

*I strongly recommend wearing gloves when handling chiles. Also be sure to wash your hands immediately after.

Combine the chiles, garlic, and salt in a food processor and pulse until the chiles are finely chopped.

Add the sugar and vinegar to the chile mixture and pulse to combine. Transfer the mixture to an airtight container and refrigerate for at least 24 hours before use. The sambal can be stored in the fridge for up to 2 months.

Ketjap

1 tablespoon canola oil

2 teaspoons minced garlic

2 teaspoons grated fresh
  ginger (from a 1-inch knob)

2 teaspoons minced seeded
  jalapeño (optional)

¼ cup packed light
  brown sugar

¼ cup tamari

½ teaspoon five-spice powder

Heat the oil in a small saucepan over medium-high heat. Stir in the garlic, ginger, and jalapeño (if using) and sauté until fragrant but not yet browned, 2 to 3 minutes. Add the brown sugar, tamari, five-spice powder, and ½ cup of water. Bring the mixture to a simmer and cook until the sauce reduces and coats the back of a spoon, about 10 minutes. Remove from the heat. The ketjap can be stored in the fridge for 2 weeks.

Fresno Chile Hot Sauce

1 pound Fresno chiles,
  roughly chopped*

5 garlic cloves, smashed

2 shallots, roughly chopped

1 cup rice vinegar

1 cup apple cider vinegar

1 teaspoon smoked paprika

1½ teaspoons sugar

1 teaspoon kosher salt

*I strongly recommend wearing gloves while handling chiles. Be sure to wash your hands immediately after. Feel free to remove the seeds for a less-spicy hot sauce.

Combine the chiles, garlic, shallots, rice vinegar, apple cider vinegar, 1 cup of water, smoked paprika, sugar, and salt in a Dutch oven. Bring the mixture to a boil over high heat, then reduce the heat to low, cover, and simmer until the vegetables are softened, about 20 minutes. Remove from the heat.

Using caution as the mixture will be very hot, carefully transfer the mixture to a high-powered blender. Holding the top securely down, start blending on low speed and gradually increase the speed to medium-high until the sauce is smooth. Let cool completely.

Once cooled, strain the hot sauce through a fine-mesh strainer. Transfer to jars or bottles and store in the fridge for up to 2 weeks.

Easy Garlic Chili Crisp

3 shallots

10 garlic cloves

½ cup red pepper flakes

½ teaspoon smoked paprika

1 teaspoon kosher salt

1 teaspoon light or dark brown sugar

1⅓ cups neutral oil, such as avocado oil, grapeseed oil, or corn oil

1 tablespoon toasted sesame seeds

1 tablespoon low-sodium soy sauce

Slice the shallots and garlic into ⅛-inch slices. Cutting them the same thickness will ensure they cook evenly. The best way to achieve an even and consistent thickness is to carefully slice everything using a mandoline.

Whisk together the pepper flakes, smoked paprika, salt, and brown sugar in a heatproof bowl (metal works best; glass could crack). Set aside.

Combine the oil, garlic, and shallots in a medium saucepan over medium heat. Cook, stirring constantly, until the shallots and garlic are golden brown, 10 to 15 minutes. The oil will begin to foam as it heats up and it may be hard to see the garlic and shallots, so be sure to keep stirring. This will also help them cook evenly. Once the shallots and garlic are ready, remove them from the heat and carefully transfer the entire mixture to the bowl with the pepper flakes. Stir to combine. The bowl will heat up once the hot oil has been added, so use caution when touching the bowl.

Add the sesame seeds and soy sauce and stir to combine. Let the mixture cool completely. Store in an airtight container in the fridge for up to 3 months.

Mild Blender Salsa

One 14.5-ounce can diced tomatoes

½ small red onion

⅓ cup packed cilantro leaves

Juice of 1 lime

1 teaspoon kosher salt

Combine the tomatoes, onion, cilantro, lime juice, and salt in a blender and blend on medium until the mixture is smooth. Store in an airtight container in the fridge for up to 1 week.

Cajun Hollandaise Sauce

10 tablespoons
  unsalted butter

1 tablespoon freshly squeezed
  lemon juice

5 large egg yolks

1 tablespoon Cajun seasoning

Melt the butter in a small saucepan over medium heat. Once the solids have separated and sunk to the bottom, remove the pan from the heat.

Combine the lemon juice, egg yolks, and Cajun seasoning in a blender and blend on medium speed until the sauce has slightly lightened in color. With the motor running, slowly add the melted butter, leaving the solids in the pan. Increase the speed to high for a few seconds to thoroughly combine. Add a little bit of hot water to thin the sauce to a nice, spoonable consistency. Serve immediately while warm.

Tartar Sauce

1 cup mayonnaise

2 tablespoons finely chopped
  dill pickle or relish

1 tablespoon chopped dill

1 tablespoon freshly squeezed
  lemon juice

Kosher salt and freshly
  ground black pepper

Combine the mayo, pickle, dill, and lemon juice in a medium bowl. Season to taste with salt and pepper. Cover and refrigerate for at least 1 hour and up to 2 days.

Sugar-Free
Ketchup
(page 318)

Cajun
Hollandaise
(page 331)

Silky Blender
Pesto (page 337)

Go-To Gravy
(page 335)

Classic Pesto
(page 336)

Tartar Sauce
(page 331)

Marinara Sauce
(page 335)

Garlic Confit
(page 319)

Cilantro Pesto
(page 336)

Mild Blender
Salsa (page 330)

Tapenade

1 cup pitted
   Castelvetrano olives

½ cup pitted kalamata olives

¼ cup parsley leaves

¼ cup basil leaves

1 garlic clove, grated

2 tablespoons freshly
   squeezed lemon juice

¼ cup extra virgin olive oil

½ teaspoon anchovy paste

Kosher salt and freshly
   ground black pepper

Combine the olives, parsley, basil, garlic, lemon juice, olive oil, and anchovy paste in a food processor and pulse until everything is finely chopped but still has some texture. Season to taste with salt and pepper. Store in an airtight container in the fridge for up to 2 weeks.

Easy Tzatziki

1 cup Greek yogurt

1 Persian cucumber, finely
   diced (about ⅓ cup)

2 tablespoons chopped dill

1 small garlic clove, grated

2 tablespoons freshly
   squeezed lemon juice

1 tablespoon extra virgin
   olive oil

Kosher salt and freshly
   ground black pepper

Combine the yogurt, cucumber, dill, garlic, lemon juice, olive oil, ½ teaspoon salt, and ¼ teaspoon pepper in a bowl. Mix until evenly combined. Season to taste with salt and pepper. Serve immediately or cover and store in the fridge for up to 3 days.

Go-To Gravy

3 cups low-sodium chicken
  stock (or turkey or
  beef stock)

2 thyme sprigs

3 tablespoons unsalted butter

3 tablespoons all-
  purpose flour

Kosher salt and freshly
  ground black pepper

Freshly squeezed lemon juice,
  as needed

Bring the stock and thyme to a simmer in a medium saucepan over medium-low heat.

Melt the butter in a medium straight-sided skillet over medium-high heat. Add the flour and cook, whisking frequently, until the mixture is light brown in color, 5 to 10 minutes (for a darker gravy, cook the flour to a deeper brown).

Whisking constantly, add 2 cups of the warm stock and cook until the gravy thickens and bubbles. Add more stock if a thinner consistency is desired. Reduce the heat to low and season to taste with salt and pepper. Add a squeeze of lemon juice and taste again for seasoning.

Keep warm until ready to serve, adding more warm stock as needed. Pour into a gravy boat and serve.

Marinara Sauce

⅓ cup extra virgin olive oil

6 garlic cloves, minced

Three 26-ounce cartons
  chopped tomatoes

1 teaspoon Italian seasoning

1 large basil sprig

Kosher salt and freshly
  ground black pepper

3 tablespoons unsalted butter

Heat the olive oil in a large saucepan over medium heat. Add the garlic and cook, stirring frequently, just until it turns golden, 3 to 4 minutes. Add the tomatoes, Italian seasoning, basil, 1 teaspoon salt, and a few grinds of fresh pepper. Bring to a simmer and cook, stirring occasionally, for 7 minutes.

Remove from the heat and stir in the butter until melted. Season to taste with salt and pepper. After cooling, store any extra marinara in an airtight container in the fridge for up to 1 week or in the freezer for up to 6 months.

Classic Pesto

1 bunch fresh basil (about
   3 cups leaves)

½ cup freshly grated
   Parmesan (about 2 ounces)

3 tablespoons toasted
   pine nuts

1 garlic clove, smashed

½ cup extra virgin olive oil,
   plus more as needed

2 tablespoons freshly
   squeezed lemon juice

Kosher salt and freshly
   ground black pepper

Combine the basil, Parmesan, pine nuts, and garlic in a food processor. Pulse a few times to break up the garlic and nuts. Add ¼ cup of the oil and pulse a few more times, stopping to scrape down the sides as needed. With the machine running, stream in the remaining ¼ cup olive oil and the lemon juice until a thick paste forms. Season to taste with salt and pepper and pulse a few more times to combine.

Transfer the pesto to an airtight container. Cover with a thin layer of olive oil to prevent browning. Store in the fridge for up to 2 days or in the freezer in an airtight container for up to 9 months. To serve with pasta, see the instructions on page 337.

Cilantro Pesto

½ cup extra virgin olive oil,
   plus more as needed

1 garlic clove, smashed

1 tablespoon lime zest (from
   1 to 2 limes)

3 tablespoons freshly
   squeezed lime juice (from
   1 to 2 limes)

¼ teaspoon red pepper flakes

2 cups packed cilantro leaves

¾ cup roasted
   unsalted cashews

½ cup crumbled cotija

Kosher salt and freshly
   ground black pepper

Combine the olive oil, garlic, lime zest and juice, and pepper flakes in a food processor and pulse together until the garlic is finely chopped. Add the cilantro and blend until smooth. Add the cashews and cotija and pulse until the mixture becomes a thick paste and is evenly combined. Add salt and pepper to taste and pulse a few more times to combine. Stream in more oil if a thinner sauce is desired.

Transfer the pesto to an airtight container. Cover with a thin layer of olive oil to prevent browning. Store in the fridge for up to 2 days.

This pesto is great tossed with vegetables or pasta, served with meat or fish, or used in dressings. To serve with pasta, see the instructions on page 337.

Silky Blender Pesto

4 cups lightly packed
    basil leaves

½ cup pine nuts

1 garlic clove, smashed

¼ teaspoon kosher salt

¼ teaspoon freshly ground
    black pepper

⅔ cup extra virgin olive oil,
    plus more as needed

¾ cup freshly grated Pecorino
    (about 3 ounces)

¾ cup freshly grated
    Parmesan (about 3 ounces),
    plus more for garnish,
    if desired

Place the basil leaves in a large bowl, cover with cold water, and let sit while you start the pesto.

Combine the pine nuts, garlic, salt, pepper, and ⅓ cup of the olive oil in a blender. Blend on high speed until the mixture is smooth and looks like a liquidy nut butter. Drain the basil leaves, but do not pat them dry. The excess water will help create a smooth and silky sauce. Add the basil leaves to the blender along with the remaining ⅓ cup olive oil and blend on medium to high speed until completely smooth. Add the cheeses and blend on medium to high speed until just combined.

Transfer the pesto to an airtight container. Cover with a thin layer of olive oil to prevent browning. Store in the fridge for up to 2 days.

To serve with pasta, make 1 pound pasta of choice. Cook according to the package directions and reserve 1 cup of pasta water. Drain the pasta and return it to the pot and add the pesto and ½ cup of reserved pasta water. Stir together until smooth and creamy, adding more pasta water as needed.

Indulge

THE SHOPPING LIST

- ☐ Indulge in real butter
- ☐ Indulge in the freshest fruits and vegetables
- ☐ Indulge in something new
- ☐ Indulge in a good long walk
- ☐ Indulge in the changing seasons
- ☐ Indulge in music
- ☐ Indulge in the stars
- ☐ Indulge in the moon
- ☐ Indulge in silence
- ☐ Indulge in a good book
- ☐ Indulge in your heartbeat (listen, marvel, appreciate)
- ☐ Indulge in a smile (yours and others)
- ☐ Indulge in remembering your best moment when you're at your worst
- ☐ Indulge in lending a hand to those who need it
- ☐ Indulge in the difference between need and want (and the large gap between the two)
- ☐ Indulge in a job well done
- ☐ Indulge in a purposeful effort

- ☐ Indulge in the morning air
- ☐ Indulge in a cup of coffee
- ☐ Indulge in a favorite cookie (while it's fresh from the oven)
- ☐ Indulge in a dinner party for friends
- ☐ Indulge in a fancy soap
- ☐ Indulge in laughter
- ☐ Indulge in a phone call to a friend
- ☐ Indulge in a hug with your kid (you did that; yes, you did)
- ☐ Indulge in travel
- ☐ Indulge in the beauty of the natural world
- ☐ Indulge in kindness
- ☐ Indulge in generosity
- ☐ Indulge in spirit
- ☐ Indulge in faith
- ☐ Indulge in love
- ☐ Indulge in gratitude
- ☐ Indulge in the moment, this very moment, right now, and try to make it a great one (cheers to you . . . to us!)

Special Ingredients

A book like this requires a lot of cooks in the kitchen, if you will, and I was fortunate to collaborate with a bunch of all-stars, including my queen of multitasking, culinary producer, recipe developer, and food stylist Sophie Clark, without whom I couldn't have done this book; also David Boyle, Megan Hubbell, and Alyssa Montes Garcia, who assisted in the kitchen and worked with me on *Valerie's Home Cooking*; Deborah Dupree, our set decorator; photographer John Russo and his phenomenal team, who took all the gorgeous food and lifestyle photos; and my longtime glam squad and pals Kimmie Urgel and Lisa Ashley. Thank you! Then there's Todd Gold, my sweet and funny storytelling friend of forty years. No book gets written without you. Here's to another forty.

I want to thank my very patient editor at HarperCollins, Deb Brody, for pushing me to "indulge" in this cookbook immediately after publishing my previous book, *Enough Already*. I think she had a vision for it before I did, but I subsequently found the months of work to be very therapeutic while I was also navigating my way through a challenging divorce. It wasn't easy, but I took it day by day and came out the other end feeling stronger and wiser.

My gratitude goes out to Deb's entire Harvest/HarperCollins team: assistant editor Emma Effinger, senior designer Tai Blanche and senior art director Mumtaz Mustafa (the book really is beautiful!), production editorial manager Rachel Meyers, copy editor Heather Rodino (thanks for the great notes and support!), associate publicity director Lindsey Kennedy, and marketing director Allison Carney.

I want to also thank my literary agent, Trident Media Group CEO Dan Strone, who has shepherded me through six books now (and I'm looking forward to writing more), and his TMG associate, Claire Romine. Likewise, Marc Schwartz and Jack Grossbart, who do the work so I can work—and do it with taste, devotion, and humor that is a gift all its own.

I could fill many, many pages with names of more people who are important to me professionally and personally, from my lawyer and business manager to my family and friends, but I have in mind keeping this relatively short and sweet, so let me simply say thank you, thank you, thank you to everyone who has stuck by me and encouraged me and indulged me with your love and kindness and faith, especially when I had trouble finding it in myself. My heart is full of your love and friendship.

Finally, I want to thank you, the reader. You've cooked my recipes, read my books, watched my shows and movies, and even stopped me in the grocery store to say hi. Most of you have been with me since the beginning of my career, and I wouldn't be here without your support, kindness, and belief. I get to indulge in what I love to do because of you. Many of you tell me that you've grown up with me. But I've grown up with you, too. I love the community we've created, bonding over issues large and small, and important and trivial, as friends do. You give me so much grace, and I want you to know it's appreciated.

When I was younger, back in the '70s when I wore bell bottoms, went barefoot, and clipped a strand of puka shells around my neck, I would say goodbye to people with a simple word that I will say to you now, until we get together again: Peace.

XO

Valerie

Universal Conversion Chart

OVEN TEMPERATURE EQUIVALENTS

250°F = 120°C

275°F = 135°C

300°F = 150°C

325°F = 160°C

350°F = 180°C

375°F = 190°C

400°F = 200°C

425°F = 220°C

450°F = 230°C

475°F = 240°C

500°F = 260°C

MEASUREMENT EQUIVALENTS

Measurements should always be level
unless directed otherwise.

⅛ teaspoon = 0.5 mL

¼ teaspoon = 1 mL

½ teaspoon = 2 mL

1 teaspoon = 5 mL

1 tablespoon = 3 teaspoons = ½ fluid ounce = 15 mL

2 tablespoons = ⅛ cup = 1 fluid ounce = 30 mL

4 tablespoons = ¼ cup = 2 fluid ounces = 60 mL

5⅓ tablespoons = ⅓ cup = 3 fluid ounces = 80 mL

8 tablespoons = ½ cup = 4 fluid ounces = 120 mL

10⅔ tablespoons = ⅔ cup = 5 fluid ounces = 160 mL

12 tablespoons = ¾ cup = 6 fluid ounces = 180 mL

16 tablespoons = 1 cup = 8 fluid ounces = 240 mL

Index

A

affogato, 292
anchovies, Bagna Cauda and Crudités, 52
antioxidants, 159, 282
antipasto, Roasted Antipasto with Crostini, 64
appetizers. *See* snacks and appetizers
asparagus, Charred Asparagus, 155

B

Baby Kale with Crispy Garlic, 151
Bacon Jam, 307, 308
Bacon-Wrapped Jalapeño Poppers, 50
Bagna Cauda and Crudités, 52
Baguette Snacks, 55–56
Baked Potato Chips, 227
Baked Sweet Potato Fries, 224
bananas
  Banana Cottage Cheese Pancakes, 11
  Brown Butter Banana Walnut Muffins, 8
  Peanut Butter, Banana, and Honey Sandwich, 40
  Pisang Goreng, 280, 292
beef. *See* meat
Beef and Broccoli, 203
Bertinelli, David, 251
Bertinelli, Patrick, 279
Bertinelli, Stacy, 279
Bertinelli Bread Dough, 117, 122–123
Beverly Hills Chopped Salad, 78
Blackened Catfish Sandwiches, 235
Blistered Green Beans, 152
Blueberry Clafoutis, 282
Blue Cheese Dressing, 321, 323
bone broth, Ginger Turmeric Bone Broth, 137

bread, 116–131
  Bertinelli Bread Dough, 117, 122–123
  Brown Butter Banana Walnut Muffins, 8
  Chive Popovers, 124
  Milk Bread, 128
  Multigrain Cinnamon Raisin Bread, 120–121
  Multigrain Seeded Bread, 126–127
  Nonnie's Crescia, 118–119
  Pretzel Buns, 130
breakfast, 7–23
  Banana Cottage Cheese Pancakes, 11
  Brown Butter Banana Walnut Muffins, 8
  Classic Eggs Benedict, 13
  Eggs in Purgatory with Kale, 14
  Everyday Smoothie, 16
  Ham, Spinach, and Broccoli Omelet, 18
  Maple Pecan Scones, 20
  Wolfie's Egg Bites, 23
broccoli
  Beef and Broccoli, 203
  Ham, Spinach, and Broccoli Omelet, 18
  Roasted Broccoli and Garlic Pasta, 266
Brown Butter Banana Walnut Muffins, 8
Bub & Grandma's, 114
Burrata with Grilled Peaches, 76
Burton, Kia, 106, 107
Burton, Tyler, 106, 107

C

cabbage
  Pork Chops with Cabbage and Apple, 212
  Roasted Cabbage, 148, 163
Café Americain, 36

Cajun Hollandaise Sauce, 331, 332
Calabrian Chili Shrimp on Toast, 236
Calabrian Chili Vinaigrette, 323, 328
California Cobb, 80
Caprese Baguette, 55
Carrot Ginger Loaf, 285
catfish, Blackened Catfish Sandwiches, 235
cauliflower, Roasted Cauliflower and Garlic Soup, 143
charcuterie. *See* cheese and charcuterie
Charred Asparagus, 155
cheese, 106–107
  Blue Cheese Dressing, 321, 323
  Crispy Goat Cheese Salad, 88
  Four-Cheese Baked Ziti, 262
  Ham and Brie Sandwiches on Pretzel Buns, 26, 36
  Sausage and Olive Cheese Bites, 67
  Spinach Ricotta Grilled Cheese, 42
  Zesty Cheddar Cheese Crackers, 65
cheese and charcuterie, 108–113
  charcuterie how-to, 112
  cheese board how-to, 110
  cooked cured meats/spreads, 112
  dry-cured meats, 112
  extras, 110, 112
  firm cheese, 110
  hard cheese, 110
  rules, 110, 112
  salami, 112
  semisoft cheese, 110
  soft cheese, 110
The Cheesemonger, 106
chicken, 170–199
  Chicken Breasts with Tomato Prosecco Sauce, 172–173
  Chicken Chili with Poblanos and Corn, 134
  Chicken Salad, 83

chicken (*continues*)
  Chicken Thigh Parm, 174
  Cornish Hens with Wild Rice
    Stuffing, 176–177
  Crispy Chicken Thighs with
    Radishes and Fennel, 178–179
  Ginger Miso Chicken Wrap, 180
  Gumbo-Inspired Chicken Thighs
    and Rice, 183
  Honey Ginger Chicken Wings, 184
  Jalapeño Popper Chicken
    Breasts, 187
  Kumquat Ginger Braised Chicken
    Thighs, 188
  Lemon Pepper Chicken Wings, 190
  Meal Prep Grilled Chicken Breasts,
    170, 191
  Mediterranean Chicken Thighs with
    Potatoes, Peppers, and Feta, 193
  Mom's Roasted Chicken and
    Vegetables, 194
  One-Pan Honey Mustard Chicken
    Thighs, 196–197
  Peanut Chicken with Collard
    Greens, 198
Chili Crisp Scallops and Corn, 238
Chipotle Shrimp Salad Lettuce
  Cups, 255
Chive Popovers, 124
Chocolate Nuggets, 287
Chocolate Peanut Butter Dates, 289
Cilantro Pesto, 333, 336
Citrus Curd, 307, 309
clams
  Clams Casino, 58–59
  Vongole with Sausage and
    Greens, 276
Classic Double Cheeseburger with
  Special Sauce, 204
Classic Eggs Benedict, 13
Classic Hummus, 60
Classic Mashed Potatoes, 220
Classic Mayo, 314, 317
Classic Pesto, 332, 336
Classic Ranch Dressing, 320, 322
Coconut Poached Salmon and
  Rice, 240
cod
  Crispy Cod Sandwiches, 243
  Smoky Slow-Roasted Cod
    Puttanesca, 256
Cold Miso Peanut Zoodles, 156
Cold Poached Salmon Nicoise
  Salad, 84–85
collard greens, Peanut Chicken with
  Collard Greens, 198
condiments, dressings, and
  sauces, 313–337

Blue Cheese Dressing, 321, 323
Cajun Hollandaise Sauce, 331, 332
Calabrian Chili Vinaigrette, 323, 328
Cilantro Pesto, 333, 336
Classic Mayo, 314, 317
Classic Pesto, 332, 336
Classic Ranch Dressing, 320, 322
Creamy Italian Dressing, 321, 323
Dijon Mustard, 317, 318
Dill Pickle Vinaigrette, 322, 327
Easy Garlic Chili Crisp, 316, 330
Easy Tzatziki, 334
Fresno Chile Hot Sauce, 317, 329
Garlic Confit, 319, 333
Ginger Miso Dressing, 322, 326
Go-To Gravy, 332, 335
Green Goddess Dressing, 322, 324
Herb Mayo, 315, 317
Homemade BBQ Sauce, 316, 319
Homemade Mayo, Three
  Ways, 314–315
Honey Mustard Dressing, 323, 327
Jalapeño Ranch Dressing, 320, 322
Ketjap, 317, 329
Lemon Caesar Dressing, 323, 324
Lemon Herb Vinaigrette, 322, 325
Marinara Sauce, 333, 335
Mild Blender Salsa, 330, 333
Red Wine Vinaigrette, 323, 325
Roasted Garlic Mayo, 315, 316
Sambal Oelek, 316, 328
Shallot Dressing, 322, 326
Silky Blender Pesto, 332, 337
Sugar-Free Ketchup, 318, 332
Tapenade, 317, 334
Tartar Sauce, 331, 332
cooked cured meats/spreads, 112
cookies
  Lemon Lime White Chocolate Chip
    Cookies, 294
  Thyme and Gruyère Savory
    Cookies, 72
corn
  Chicken Chili with Poblanos and
    Corn, 134
  Chili Crisp Scallops and Corn, 238
  Elote Salad, 91
Cornish Hens with Wild Rice
  Stuffing, 176–177
cottage cheese, Banana Cottage
  Cheese Pancakes, 11
Cream Cheese Brownies, 291
Creamy Italian Dressing, 321, 323
Creamy No-Cream Artichoke Pasta, 261
creativity, 3, 5, 230
Cress Salad, 87
Crispy Chicken Thighs with Radishes
  and Fennel, 178–179

Crispy Chickpeas, 61
Crispy Cod Sandwiches, 243
Crispy Goat Cheese Salad, 88
Crispy Parmesan Potatoes, 222
Cuban Sandwich with Slow-Cooker
  Pulled Pork, 30
cured meats, 112
curiosity, 106

D
De Laurentiis, Giada, 106
dessert, 280–305
  Blueberry Clafoutis, 282
  Carrot Ginger Loaf, 285
  Chocolate Nuggets, 287
  Chocolate Peanut Butter
    Dates, 289
  Cream Cheese Brownies, 291
  Espresso Affogato, 292
  Lemon Lime White Chocolate Chip
    Cookies, 294
  No-Churn Buttermilk Vanilla Ice
    Cream, 296
  No-Churn Chocolate Peanut
    Butter Ice Cream, 298
  PB&J Cups, 300
  Pineapple Upside-Down Cake, 303
  Pisang Goreng, 280, 292
  Strawberry Pretzel Salad, 304–305
Dijon Mustard, 317, 318
Dill Pickle Vinaigrette, 322, 327
dinner for one, 168–169
dressings. See condiments,
  dressings, and sauces
dry-cured meats, 112

E
Easy Garlic Chili Crisp, 316, 330
Easy Tzatziki, 334
eggs. See breakfast
Elote Salad, 91
emotional honesty, 278
Espresso Affogato, 292
essential pleasure, food as, 2
Everyday Smoothie, 16

F
fiber, 159, 261
Filet Mignon with Béarnaise
  Sauce, 206–207
firm cheese, 110
fish. See seafood
food, as essential pleasure, 2
Food Network, 14, 106
Food & Wine magazine, 230
forgiveness, 168, 169
Four-Cheese Baked Ziti, 262
Fresno Chile Hot Sauce, 317, 329

fried bananas, 292
friendships, 2
Frisée Salad, 92

G
Garlic Confit, 319
Garlic Confit BLT, 35
Ginger Miso Chicken Wrap, 180
Ginger Miso Dressing, 322, 326
Ginger Turmeric Bone Broth, 137
girl dinners. *See* cheese and
    charcuterie
Glazed Sweet Potatoes, 159
Go-To Gravy, 332, 335
grandmother
    adaption of recipe
    belonging to, 209
    memories of, 3
    recipe passed down by, 118, 122
Grant, Taylor, 230
Grapefruit Salad, 94
gratitude, 278–279
green beans, Blistered Green
    Beans, 152
Green Goddess Dressing, 322, 324
Guarnaschelli, Alex, 106
Gumbo-Inspired Chicken Thighs
    and Rice, 183

H
Ham and Brie Sandwiches on Pretzel
    Buns, 26, 36
Ham and Butter Baguette, 55
Ham, Spinach, and Broccoli
    Omelet, 18
hard cheese, 110
Harris, Jenn, 25
Herb Mayo, 315, 317
Homemade BBQ Sauce, 316, 319
Homemade Mayo, Three
    Ways, 314–315
Homemade Peanut Butter, 307, 310
Homemade Potato Chips with
    Chicken Salt, 228
Honey Ginger Chicken Wings, 184
Honey Mustard Dressing, 323, 327
honeys. *See* jams, spreads,
    and honeys
Hot in Cleveland, 20
Hot Honey, 307, 308
hummus, Classic Hummus, 60

I
ice cream
    No-Churn Buttermilk Vanilla Ice
    Cream, 296
    No-Churn Chocolate Peanut
    Butter Ice Cream, 298

inspiration, finding, 3, 4, 115
Italian Meatloaf, 209

J
Jalapeño Popper Chicken
    Breasts, 187
Jalapeño Ranch Dressing, 320, 322
jams, spreads and honeys, 306–311
    Bacon Jam, 307, 308
    Citrus Curd, 307, 309
    Homemade Peanut Butter, 307, 310
    Hot Honey, 307, 308
    Strawberry Rhubarb Jam, 307, 311
    Turmeric Ginger Honey, 307, 311
Jell-O, 304
Jenny Craig, 50
Jersey Mike's, 114
John, Elton, 24

K
Kadin, Andy, 114
kale
    Baby Kale with Crispy Garlic, 151
    Eggs in Purgatory with Kale, 14
    Kale and Sweet Potato Salad, 96
    White Bean and Kale Soup, 132, 147
ketchup, sugar-free, 318
Ketjap, 317, 329
Ketjap Sambal Marinated Rib Eye, 211
Kids Baking Championship (Food
    Network), 14
Kumquat Ginger Braised Chicken
    Thighs, 188

L
La Scala restaurant, 78
laughter, 278
Lazy No-Bake Lasagna, 265
Leeves, Jane, 20
Lefebvre, Ludo, 92, 106
Lemon Caesar Dressing, 324
Lemon Herb Vinaigrette, 322, 325
Lemon Lime White Chocolate Chip
    Cookies, 294
Lemon Pepper Chicken Wings, 190
Lemon Whitefish with Roasted
    Fennel Slaw, 244
life lessons, 25
Loaded Miso Soup, 138
Los Angeles Times, 25
love, 168

M
Mammoth (band), 23
Maple Pecan Scones, 20
Marinara Sauce, 333, 335
mayo, homemade, 314–315
Mazzeo, Rosario, 25

McDonald's, 243
Meal Prep Grilled Chicken Breasts,
    170, 191
measurement equivalents, 340
meat, 200–217
    Beef and Broccoli, 203
    Classic Double Cheeseburger with
    Special Sauce, 204
    Filet Mignon with Béarnaise
    Sauce, 206–207
    Italian Meatloaf, 209
    Ketjap Sambal Marinated Rib
    Eye, 211
    Pork Chops with Cabbage and
    Apple, 212
    Prime Rib with Horseradish
    Sauce, 215
    Slow-Cooker Pulled Pork with
    Shallots and Chiles, 216
    Spaghetti and Meatballs,
    272–273
meats, cured, 112
Mediterranean Chicken Thighs
    with Potatoes, Peppers, and
    Feta, 193
menu planning, 114–115
Mild Blender Salsa, 330, 333
Milk Bread, 128
Mom's Hero, 39
Mom's Roasted Chicken and
    Vegetables, 194
Mom's Waldorf Salad, 98
mother
    adaption of recipe
    belonging to, 209
    go-to dish belonging to, 194
    memories of, 3, 24–25, 39, 120
muffins, Brown Butter
    Banana Walnut Muffins, 8
Multigrain Cinnamon Raisin
    Bread, 120–121
Multigrain Seeded Bread, 126–127

N
New York Times, 274
1970s Special Turkey Sandwich,
    28
No-Churn Buttermilk Vanilla Ice
    Cream, 296
No-Churn Chocolate Peanut Butter
    Ice Cream, 298
Nonnie's Crescia, 118–119

O
One-Pan Honey Mustard Chicken
    Thighs, 196–197
Oven-"Fried" Okra, 62
oven temperature equivalents, 340

P

pancakes, Banana Cottage Cheese Pancakes, 11
pasta, 259–277
  Creamy No-Cream Artichoke Pasta, 261
  Four-Cheese Baked Ziti, 262
  Lazy No-Bake Lasagna, 265
  Roasted Broccoli and Garlic Pasta, 266
  Shrimp Scampi Pasta with Herb Bread Crumbs, 268
  Spaghetti al Limone, 270
  Spaghetti and Meatballs, 272–273
  Vegetable Bolognese with Spaghetti Squash, 274–275
  Vongole with Sausage and Greens, 276
PB&J Cups, 300
peaches, Burrata with Grilled Peaches, 76
Peanut Butter, Banana, and Honey Sandwich, 40
Peanut Chicken with Collard Greens, 198
People magazine, 106
Pepperidge Farm, 285
Petite Trois, 92
Pineapple Upside-Down Cake, 303
Pisang Goreng, 280, 292
pork
  Cuban Sandwich with Slow-Cooker Pulled Pork, 30
  Pork Chops with Cabbage and Apple, 212
  Slow-Cooker Pulled Pork with Shallots and Chiles, 216
potatoes, 218–229
  Baked Potato Chips, 227
  Baked Sweet Potato Fries, 224
  Classic Mashed Potatoes, 220
  Crispy Parmesan Potatoes, 222
  Homemade Potato Chips with Chicken Salt, 228
  Turkey Cottage Pie, 219, 229
Pretzel Buns, 130
Prime Rib with Horseradish Sauce, 215

Q

Quick Turkey and Butternut Squash Soup, 140

R

Ratatouille, 161
Ray, Rachael, 265
Red Wine Vinaigrette, 323, 325
Reese's Peanut Butter Cups, 300

Refrigerator Pickled Vegetables, 48, 57
relationship with food, 2
Roasted Antipasto with Crostini, 64
Roasted Broccoli and Garlic Pasta, 266
Roasted Cabbage, 148, 163
Roasted Cauliflower and Garlic Soup, 143
Roasted Garlic Mayo, 315, 316
Roasted Tomato Panzanella, 100
Roasted Tomato Soup with Garlic Bread Croutons, 144–146
Romaine Heart Caesar, 103

S

salads, 75–105
  Beverly Hills Chopped Salad, 78
  Burrata with Grilled Peaches, 76
  California Cobb, 80
  Chicken Salad, 83
  Chipotle Shrimp Salad Lettuce Cups, 255
  Cold Poached Salmon Nicoise Salad, 84–85
  Cress Salad, 87
  Crispy Goat Cheese Salad, 88
  Elote Salad, 91
  Frisée Salad, 92
  Grapefruit Salad, 94
  Kale and Sweet Potato Salad, 96
  Mom's Waldorf Salad, 98
  Roasted Tomato Panzanella, 100
  Romaine Heart Caesar, 103
  Three-Bean Salad on Toast, 104
salami, 112
salmon
  Coconut Poached Salmon and Rice, 240
  Cold Poached Salmon Nicoise Salad, 84–85
  Salmon Burgers with Quick-Pickled Vegetables, 246
  Smoky Salmon Dip, 69
Sambal Oelek, 316, 328
sandwiches, 26–47
  Blackened Catfish Sandwiches, 235
  Classic Double Cheeseburger with Special Sauce, 204
  craving for, 24–25
  Crispy Cod Sandwiches, 243
  Cuban Sandwich with Slow-Cooker Pulled Pork, 30
  Egg Salad Sandwich, 33
  Garlic Confit BLT, 35
  Ham and Brie Sandwiches on Pretzel Buns, 26, 36
  Mom's Hero, 39

1970s Special Turkey Sandwich, 28
Peanut Butter, Banana, and Honey Sandwich, 40
Salmon Burgers with Quick-Pickled Vegetables, 246
Spinach Ricotta Grilled Cheese, 42
A Trio of Tea Sandwiches, 44
Tuna Salad Sandwich, 47
sauces. See condiments, dressings, and sauces
Sausage and Olive Cheese Bites, 67
Savory Snap Peas and Mushrooms, 165
scallops, Chili Crisp Scallops and Corn, 238
scones, Maple Pecan Scones, 20
seafood, 233–257
  Blackened Catfish Sandwiches, 235
  Calabrian Chili Shrimp on Toast, 236
  Chili Crisp Scallops and Corn, 238
  Chipotle Shrimp Salad Lettuce Cups, 255
  Coconut Poached Salmon and Rice, 240
  Crispy Cod Sandwiches, 243
  Lemon Whitefish with Roasted Fennel Slaw, 244
  Salmon Burgers with Quick-Pickled Vegetables, 246
  Seafood Rolls, 249
  Seafood Tomato Sauce with Crusty Bread, 251
  Shrimp Scampi Pasta with Herb Bread Crumbs, 268
  Shrimp and Veggie Lettuce Cups, 252
  Smoky Slow-Roasted Cod Puttanesca, 256
  Vongole with Sausage and Greens, 276
self-indulgence, 3
semisoft cheese, 110
shakshuka, 14
Shallot Dressing, 322, 326
shopping list (for indulging), 338
shrimp
  Calabrian Chili Shrimp on Toast, 236
  Chipotle Shrimp Salad Lettuce Cups, 255
  Shrimp Scampi Pasta with Herb Bread Crumbs, 268
  Shrimp and Veggie Lettuce Cups, 252
  Steakhouse Shrimp Cocktail with Sauce Trio, 70
Silky Blender Pesto, 332, 337

Slow-Cooker Pulled Pork with
    Shallots and Chiles, 216
Smoky Salmon Dip, 69
Smoky Slow-Roasted Cod
    Puttanesca, 256
smoothies, Everyday Smoothie, 16
snacks and appetizers, 48–73
    Bacon-Wrapped Jalapeño
        Poppers, 50
    Bagna Cauda and Crudités, 52
    Baguette Snacks, 55–56
    Caprese Baguette, 55
    Clams Casino, 58–59
    Classic Hummus, 60
    Crispy Chickpeas, 61
    Ham and Butter Baguette, 55
    Oven-"Fried" Okra, 62
    Refrigerator Pickled
        Vegetables, 48, 57
    Roasted Antipasto with Crostini, 64
    Sausage and Olive Cheese Bites, 67
    Smoky Salmon Dip, 69
    Spring Radishes with Tzatziki, 56
    Steakhouse Shrimp Cocktail with
        Sauce Trio, 70
    Tapenade and Roasted Red Pepper
        Baguette, 56
    Thyme and Gruyère Savory
        Cookies, 72
    Zesty Cheddar Cheese
        Crackers, 65
soft cheese, 110
soups, 132–147
    Chicken Chili with Poblanos and
        Corn, 134
    Ginger Turmeric Bone Broth, 137
    Loaded Miso Soup, 138
    Quick Turkey and Butternut Squash
        Soup, 140
    Roasted Cauliflower and Garlic
        Soup, 143
    Roasted Tomato Soup with Garlic
        Bread Croutons, 144–146
    White Bean and Kale Soup, 132, 147
Spaghetti al Limone, 270
Spaghetti and Meatballs, 272–273
Spinach Ricotta Grilled Cheese, 42
spreads. See jams, spreads
    and honeys
Spring Radishes with Tzatziki, 56

squash
    Quick Turkey and Butternut Squash
        Soup, 140
    Vegetable Bolognese with
        Spaghetti Squash, 274–275
Starbucks, 20, 23
Steakhouse Shrimp Cocktail with
    Sauce Trio, 70
Strawberry Pretzel Salad, 304–305
Strawberry Rhubarb Jam, 307, 311
Subway, 114
Sugar-Free Ketchup, 318, 332
sweet potatoes
    Baked Sweet Potato Fries, 224
    Glazed Sweet Potatoes, 159
    Kale and Sweet Potato Salad, 96
sweet tooth, 279, 281
Swift, Taylor, 169

T
Tapenade, 317, 334
Tapenade and Roasted Red Pepper
    Baguette, 56
Tartar Sauce, 331, 332
Three-Bean Salad on Toast, 104
Thyme and Gruyère Savory
    Cookies, 72
TikTok, 33, 222, 289
tomatoes
    Chicken Breasts with Tomato
        Prosecco Sauce, 172–173
    Roasted Tomato Panzanella, 100
    Roasted Tomato Soup with Garlic
        Bread Croutons, 144–146
    Seafood Tomato Sauce with Crusty
        Bread, 251
A Trio of Tea Sandwiches, 44
truth, 1
Tuna Salad Sandwich, 47
turkey
    1970s Special Turkey Sandwich, 28
    Quick Turkey and Butternut Squash
        Soup, 140
    Turkey Cottage Pie, 219, 229
Turmeric Ginger Honey, 307, 311

U
umami, 138
universal conversion chart, 340
upland cress, Cress Salad, 87

V
Valerie's Home Cooking, 130, 190,
    294, 303
Van Halen (band), 13
Van Halen, Andraia, 23, 156, 249,
    279, 304
Van Halen, Ed, 13, 24, 69, 168, 198,
    206, 278
Van Halen, Mrs., 198, 203, 211, 252,
    292, 314, 328
Van Halen, Wolfie, 23, 24, 25, 30, 140,
    156, 168, 249, 266, 278, 279, 292,
    294, 304
vegetables, 148–167
    Baby Kale with Crispy Garlic, 151
    Blistered Green Beans, 152
    Charred Asparagus, 155
    Cold Miso Peanut Zoodles, 156
    Glazed Sweet Potatoes, 159
    Mom's Roasted Chicken and
        Vegetables, 194
    Ratatouille, 161
    Refrigerator Pickled
        Vegetables, 48, 57
    Roasted Cabbage, 148, 163
    Savory Snap Peas and
        Mushrooms, 165
    Vegetable Bolognese with
        Spaghetti Squash, 274–275
    Vegetable Galette, 166
vineyard, backyard, 230
Vongole with Sausage and
    Greens, 276

W
Waldorf Astoria Hotel, 98
White Bean and Kale Soup, 132, 147
whitefish, Lemon Whitefish with
    Roasted Fennel Slaw, 244
wine, 230–231
wings
    Honey Ginger Chicken Wings, 184
    Lemon Pepper Chicken Wings, 190
Wolfie's Egg Bites, 23
wraps, Ginger Miso Chicken
    Wrap, 180

Z
Zesty Cheddar Cheese Crackers, 65
zoodles (zucchini noodles), 156, 261